2

W9-AQS-621

A12902 032718

OPPOSING
VIEWPOINTS®
SERIES

Sexual Violence WITHDRAWN

Other Books of Related Interest:

Opposing Viewpoints Series
Civil Liberties
Gender Roles
Homosexuality

At Issue Series
Child Pornography
Do Abstinence Programs Work?
Self-Defense Laws

Current Controversies Series
Gays in the Military
Human Trafficking
Violence in the Media

"Congress shall make no law . . . abridging the freedom of speech, or of the press."

First Amendment to the US Constitution

The basic foundation of our democracy is the First Amendment guarantee of freedom of expression. The Opposing Viewpoints Series is dedicated to the concept of this basic freedom and the idea that it is more important to practice it than to enshrine it.

OPPOSING VIEWPOINTS® SERIES

Sexual Violence

Amanda Hiber, Book Editor

GREENHAVEN PRESS
A part of Gale, Cengage Learning

I.C.C. LIBRARY

GALE
CENGAGE Learning·

Farmington Hills, Mich • San Francisco • New York • Waterville, Maine
Meriden, Conn • Mason, Ohio • Chicago

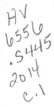

GALE
CENGAGE Learning·

Elizabeth Des Chenes, *Director, Content Strategy*
Cynthia Sanner, *Publisher*
Douglas Dentino, *Manager, New Product*

© 2014 Greenhaven Press, a part of Gale, Cengage Learning.

WCN: 01-100-101

Gale and Greenhaven Press are registered trademarks used herein under license.

For more information, contact:
Greenhaven Press
27500 Drake Rd.
Farmington Hills, MI 48331-3535
Or you can visit our Internet site at gale.cengage.com

ALL RIGHTS RESERVED.
No part of this work covered by the copyright herein may be reproduced, transmitted, stored, or used in any form or by any means graphic, electronic, or mechanical, including but not limited to photocopying, recording, scanning, digitizing, taping, Web distribution, information networks, or information storage and retrieval systems, except as permitted under Section 107 or 108 of the 1976 United States Copyright Act, without the prior written permission of the publisher.

For product information and technology assistance, contact us at

Gale Customer Support, 1-800-877-4253
For permission to use material from this text or product, submit all requests online at www.cengage.com/permissions

Further permissions questions can be emailed to permissionrequest@cengage.com

Articles in Greenhaven Press anthologies are often edited for length to meet page requirements. In addition, original titles of these works are changed to clearly present the main thesis and to explicitly indicate the author's opinion. Every effort is made to ensure that Greenhaven Press accurately reflects the original intent of the authors. Every effort has been made to trace the owners of copyrighted material.

Cover image copyright © mrkornflakes/Shutterstock.com.

LIBRARY OF CONGRESS CATALOGING-IN-PUBLICATION DATA

Sexual violence / Amanda Hiber, book editor.
    pages cm. -- (Opposing viewpoints)
    Includes bibliographical references and index.
    ISBN 978-0-7377-6340-9 (hardcover) -- ISBN 978-0-7377-6341-6 (pbk.)
    1. Sex crimes--Juvenile literature. 2. Rape--Juvenile literature. I. Hiber, Amanda.
    HV6556.S445 2014
    303.6--dc23
                                           2013036419

Printed in the United States of America
1 2 3 4 5 6 7 18 17 16 15 14

Contents

5/14 Cengage 30.95

Why Consider Opposing Viewpoints?

> *"The only way in which a human being can make some approach to knowing the whole of a subject is by hearing what can be said about it by persons of every variety of opinion and studying all modes in which it can be looked at by every character of mind. No wise man ever acquired his wisdom in any mode but this."*
>
> *John Stuart Mill*

In our media-intensive culture it is not difficult to find differing opinions. Thousands of newspapers and magazines and dozens of radio and television talk shows resound with differing points of view. The difficulty lies in deciding which opinion to agree with and which "experts" seem the most credible. The more inundated we become with differing opinions and claims, the more essential it is to hone critical reading and thinking skills to evaluate these ideas. Opposing Viewpoints books address this problem directly by presenting stimulating debates that can be used to enhance and teach these skills. The varied opinions contained in each book examine many different aspects of a single issue. While examining these conveniently edited opposing views, readers can develop critical thinking skills such as the ability to compare and contrast authors' credibility, facts, argumentation styles, use of persuasive techniques, and other stylistic tools. In short, the Opposing Viewpoints Series is an ideal way to attain the higher-level thinking and reading skills so essential in a culture of diverse and contradictory opinions.

In addition to providing a tool for critical thinking, Opposing Viewpoints books challenge readers to question their own strongly held opinions and assumptions. Most people form their opinions on the basis of upbringing, peer pressure, and personal, cultural, or professional bias. By reading carefully balanced opposing views, readers must directly confront new ideas as well as the opinions of those with whom they disagree. This is not to argue simplistically that everyone who reads opposing views will—or should—change his or her opinion. Instead, the series enhances readers' understanding of their own views by encouraging confrontation with opposing ideas. Careful examination of others' views can lead to the readers' understanding of the logical inconsistencies in their own opinions, perspective on why they hold an opinion, and the consideration of the possibility that their opinion requires further evaluation.

Evaluating Other Opinions

To ensure that this type of examination occurs, Opposing Viewpoints books present all types of opinions. Prominent spokespeople on different sides of each issue as well as well-known professionals from many disciplines challenge the reader. An additional goal of the series is to provide a forum for other, less known, or even unpopular viewpoints. The opinion of an ordinary person who has had to make the decision to cut off life support from a terminally ill relative, for example, may be just as valuable and provide just as much insight as a medical ethicist's professional opinion. The editors have two additional purposes in including these less known views. One, the editors encourage readers to respect others' opinions—even when not enhanced by professional credibility. It is only by reading or listening to and objectively evaluating others' ideas that one can determine whether they are worthy of consideration. Two, the inclusion of such viewpoints encourages the important critical thinking skill of objectively evaluating an author's credentials and bias. This evaluation will illuminate an author's reasons for taking a particular stance on an issue and will aid in readers' evaluation of the author's ideas.

It is our hope that these books will give readers a deeper understanding of the issues debated and an appreciation of the complexity of even seemingly simple issues when good and honest people disagree. This awareness is particularly important in a democratic society such as ours in which people enter into public debate to determine the common good. Those with whom one disagrees should not be regarded as enemies but rather as people whose views deserve careful examination and may shed light on one's own.

Thomas Jefferson once said that "difference of opinion leads to inquiry, and inquiry to truth." Jefferson, a broadly educated man, argued that "if a nation expects to be ignorant and free . . . it expects what never was and never will be." As individuals and as a nation, it is imperative that we consider the opinions of others and examine them with skill and discernment. The Opposing Viewpoints Series is intended to help readers achieve this goal.

David L. Bender and Bruno Leone,
Founders

Introduction

"Sexual violence profoundly affects not only the health and safety of women, but the economic and social stability of their nations."

Condoleezza Rice,
US secretary of state, United Nations
Security Council meeting, June 19, 2008

The US Centers for Disease Control and Prevention (CDC) defines sexual violence as "any sexual act that is perpetrated against someone's will" including a completed or attempted nonconsensual act, abusive sexual contact, or noncontact sexual abuse. In American culture, the types of sexual violence most often referred to are sexual abuse, particularly that of children by adults, and sexual assault, or rape. There is no federal rape law per se, however; rape is categorized with all other types of nonconsensual sexual acts. State laws against rape do exist; the main difference among which is whether force or compulsion is required to show that a rape has taken place. Eight states also require evidence of victim resistance, according to an article in the *Huffington Post*. Under these laws, someone who has consented at one point but later withdraws his or her consent is not considered a rape victim.

Internationally, there is disagreement on what constitutes sexual violence, particularly rape. Variations in definitions received much public attention when WikiLeaks founder Julian Assange was accused of rape by two different women in Sweden. One woman claims Assange forcibly raped her, while the other says she was sleeping when the assault took place. Both encounters had started out as consensual. But in Sweden, where both alleged rapes took place, continuing to have sex with someone after that person has withdrawn consent still counts as rape. Feminist writer Jessica Valenti states in the

Washington Post: "The fact that U.S. law is so ill-equipped to actually protect women in realistic scenarios is a national embarrassment—not to mention a huge hurdle in obtaining justice for sexual assault victims. Swedish rape laws . . . go much further than U.S. laws do, and we should look to them as a potential model for our own legislation."

In some countries, the existence of certain factors precludes an action being categorized as rape. Rape within marriage, for instance, was only criminalized in England in 1991 and in the United States, the final state to criminalize it, North Carolina, did not do so until 1993. But according to a 2011 United Nations report, marital rape remains legal in 127 countries, including a dozen members of the European Union. There are also several countries where the definition of rape does not allow for men to be victims or women to be assailants. In fact, the Federal Bureau of Investigation did not revise its definition of rape to include women perpetrators until 2011. At the same time, other factors, such as the age of the victim, is automatically defined as rape in many places, regardless of whether the victim claims to have consented. According to the Britain-based newsmagazine the *Economist*:

> The first recorded law on [sexual activity involving young people] was in England in 1275, which made it an offence to have sex (with or without her consent) with a "maiden within age." This was interpreted as meaning below the age of marriage, at that time 12. . . . Most countries now set the age of consent between 15 and 18 (sometimes higher for men than women) though it is as low as 13 in Spain. . . . Some countries set rules about the permitted age gap in a relationship involving a younger person whereas in others it is irrelevant.

In the United States, sexual intercourse with a minor is considered statutory rape, but various states define the age of consent differently, though all are within the range of sixteen to eighteen years of age.

Because sexual violence in most countries is subject to criminal law, its respective parameters differ significantly. But while there is disagreement about which behaviors violate which (if any) laws, there is broad agreement that sexual violence is a societal problem that must be addressed in some fashion. As with all large-scale social ills, it can only be effectively addressed after thoughtful examination. The present volume's content, arranged within chapters titled Is Sexual Violence a Widespread Problem?, What Factors Contribute to Sexual Violence?, How Does Society Respond to Sexual Violence?, and What Policies Can Help Reduce Sexual Violence?, provides a comprehensive, thoughtful, and diverse study of the scope of, the causes of, and the responses to this problem in order to facilitate such an examination, as well as the discussions and actions that it may inspire.

OPPOSING
VIEWPOINTS®
SERIES

CHAPTER 1

Is Sexual Violence a Widespread Problem?

Chapter Preface

While it is difficult to assess the accuracy of all crime statistics because of their reliance on citizens' reports, this is perhaps more true of sexual violence than of any other type of crime. The uniquely personal nature of these crimes is certainly one cause of low reporting rates, but beyond this, sexual violence victimhood often prompts feelings not associated with other crimes. Indeed, a 2003 study cited by the National Institute of Justice found that the most common reasons for not reporting sexual assaults were self-blame or guilt, shame or embarrassment, humiliation or fear of others' perceptions, fear of not being believed or of being blamed, and a lack of trust in the criminal justice system.

Fortunately, there has been a growing willingness to acknowledge these crimes in American culture in the past few decades. "During the 1970s, 1980s, and 1990s, transformations were taking place in the way Americans defined and responded to rape," writes Lauren R. Taylor in a 2006 *National Institute of Justice Journal* article. "Social and political movements—along with changes in the law—encouraged women to inform police about sex crimes." As a result of these cultural changes, criminologist Eric P. Baumer says, "During the 1970s and 1980s there was a significant increase in police notification by third parties and by victims raped by non-strangers," while at the same time, "parallel analyses of non-sexual assaults revealed no significant increase in the likelihood of police notification between 1973 and 1991." This same upward trend in reporting has occurred among child sexual abuse victims as well. According to a 2012 *New York Times* article, Crimes Against Children Research Center director Dr. David Finkelhor found in a 2008 survey that "in 50 percent of sexual abuse cases, the child's victimization had been reported to an authority, compared with 25 percent in 1992."

Despite these gains, 50 percent of occurrences of child sexual abuse continue to go unreported. At the same time, according to the Rape, Abuse & Incest National Network, approximately 54 percent of sexual assaults are never reported. Clearly, this discrepancy between the perpetration and the reporting of criminal activity renders it challenging to analyze historical trends in sexual violence and thus to respond to these crimes effectively. Still, substantial shifts in reporting rates in such a short period of time engender hope that this gap will eventually close. The authors of the viewpoints in this chapter debate the extent of sexual violence in US society.

> *"The problem is not one of isolated, random sexual assaults by errant priests but is occurring on a widespread and systematic basis throughout the church."*

Sexual Abuse of Children by Catholic Priests Is Widespread

Center for Constitutional Rights

The following viewpoint was submitted to the International Criminal Court by the Center for Constitutional Rights on behalf of the Survivors Network of those Abused by Priests, a network of victims of religious sexual abuse. This Victims' Communication, delivered as part of a request to the International Criminal Court to investigate and prosecute high-level Vatican officials, asserts that the widespread and systematic sexual violence against children and vulnerable adults by clergy continued, in large part, because of policies and practices that placed the protection of church officials above that of abuse victims.

As you read, consider the following questions:

1. According to the author, what is the harm in referring to acts of sexual violence perpetrated in the Church as "abuse"?

"Victims' Communication Pursuant to Article 15 of the Rome Statute Requesting Investigation and Prosecution of High-level Vatican Officials for Rape and Other Forms of Sexual Violence as Crimes Against Humanity and Torture as a Crime Against Humanity," Center for Constitutional Rights, September 13, 2011. Reproduced by permission.

2. Why does the author only refer to abuse victims as survivors "advisedly"?

3. In what year did the Statute of the International Criminal Court go into effect, according to the author?

In recent years, ongoing revelations of pervasive and serious sexual violence against children and vulnerable adults by priests and others associated with the Catholic church in different parts of the world have demonstrated that the problem is not one of isolated, random sexual assaults by errant priests but is occurring on a widespread and systematic basis throughout the church. In the wake of scandals in Canada, Ireland, the United States and elsewhere, experts and investigators who have carefully studied the issue and the evidence have identified policies and practices that allowed the sexual violence to occur and continue and that furthered the harm to direct victims. One after another, the investigations have found intentional cover-ups and affirmative steps taken that serve to perpetuate the violence and exacerbate the harm. The same or similar practices and policies have been found virtually everywhere that cases of sexual violence have been brought to light—in Australia, Austria, Belgium, France, Germany, Italy, the Netherlands, and Mexico among others. . . .

High-level Vatican officials, including Cardinal Joseph Ratzinger, now Pope Benedict XVI,[1] either knew and/or in some cases consciously disregarded information that showed subordinates were committing or about to commit such crimes. The persons identified herein as persons whose roles should be investigated are those high-ranking officials at the church's center of gravity—the Vatican. . . .

The Vatican is a highly centralized and hierarchical institute with all authority leading to and ultimately residing in

---

1. Pope Benedict XVI resigned on February 28, 2013, the first pontiff to do so in six hundred years. Many people speculate that his resignation was related to the sex abuse scandal.

the Pope in Rome. The persons ... in positions of power within the church [who] have implemented papal policies and laws and have exercised authority over these matters at one time or other ... bear the greatest responsibility for the system that fosters and allows sexual violence.

The Church Has Chosen Secrecy

Time and again church officials have chosen the path of secrecy and protecting their ranks over the safety and physical and mental well-being of children and vulnerable adults, families of victims and their communities.... There are documented cases showing that church officials have gone so far as to obstruct justice and/or destroy evidence in national legal systems and to have consistently engaged in the practice of 'priest shifting,' *i.e.* transferring known offenders to other locations where they continued to have access to children or vulnerable adults and who officials knew continued to commit rape and other acts of sexual violence.... There are documented cases of bishops and cardinals purposefully misleading their parishioners and communities about offending priests, lying to victims and their families, and indeed blaming victims and/or their families. Whistleblowers have been punished, and those who have endeavored to maintain secrecy and protect the institution have been rewarded.... It is now clear that the actions of such bishops and cardinals conform to, rather than depart from, Vatican policy. In doing so, they have not just kept rape and sexual violence quiet, they have kept it going.

Trivialising Language

It is important to note at the outset that often the acts of rape and sexual violence in this context are referred to as "abuse." Descriptions such as 'sexual abuse' minimize the seriousness of the conduct at issue as though it is something other than torture, rape or serious sexual violence when committed by priests or others associated with the church. A Grand Jury in Philadelphia noted this tendency and reaffirmed the multi-dimensional effects and gravity of all forms of sexual violence in this context:

> We should begin by making one thing clear. When we say abuse, we don't just mean "inappropriate touching" (as the Archdiocese often chose to refer to it). We mean rape. Boys who were raped orally, boys who were raped anally, girls who were raped vaginally. *But even those victims whose physical abuse did not include actual rape—those who were subjected to fondling, to masturbation, to pornography—suffered psychological abuse that scarred their lives and sapped the faith in which they had been raised.* (emphasis added)

A report issued by experts in Germany also noted this tendency:

> With regard to the misconduct in question, namely the sexual offences, it must be emphasized that euphemistic, trivialising language was used, which, from the point of view of the experts, often gave no more than an inkling of the complete extent of the offence and its effect on the victim.

Profound Effects

A study conducted by the John Jay College of Criminal Justice [in New York City] ... found that of the more than 10,000 credible allegations of 'child sexual abuse' reported to church officials in the U.S. between the years 1950 and 2002, a large percentage involved penile penetration or attempted penile penetration or oral sex, acts which constitute rape, attempted rape or sexual violence.

Such terminology masks the true extent of the harm such acts cause and the severe pain and suffering associated with the abuse of power, violation of trust and bodily autonomy, as well as the alienation and isolation from family, friends, community, and other sources of support. Especially for children, such acts can separate them from their sense of connection to their family, the spiritual community and foundations through which they are taught to view the world and, indeed, the world itself. One Polish survivor of rape described this dynamic as feeling as though *"we've lost our grounding on Earth."*

Indeed, the gravity of the harm is such that while we use the term "survivor" where appropriate ... to acknowledge, affirm and empower those to whom such violence has been done, we do so advisedly. As is tragically demonstrated in the reports and investigations ... many have not survived their experiences. The reports ... document tragic cases of suicides and attempted suicides as a result of not only the sexual violence inflicted on the victims but the psychological violence, including the alienation and isolation, inflicted by the Church in the aftermath—the brutality involved in a system that knowingly exposes and subjects children and vulnerable adults to violent acts and then protects the perpetrators while turning its back on and condemning the victims.

The Cover-up Continues

There has been much talk of "reforms" and "zero tolerance" policies by church officials over the past few years. As recent commissions of inquiry and grand jury findings ... demonstrate, sexual violence is still being committed within the church with impunity and the priest-shifting and cover-ups are still happening, also with impunity.... Five recent cases of individual complainants ... confirm that the sexual violence is still happening and that the policy and practice of those at the seat of power have not changed. The reforms have been largely cosmetic and have left intact the system of cover-up and secrecy that perpetuates the violence....

Evidence of offenses that may have occurred outside the court's territorial or temporal jurisdiction is widely available and useful to further establish the threshold requirements of

Personal Familiarity with Abuse Among Catholics

Percent respondents who personally know:

	Someone abused by a priest	A priest accused of abuse
Total Catholics	7%	12%
Period:		
Pre-Vatican II	10%	19%
Vatican II	9%	16%
Post-Vatican II	7%	9%
Millennial	4%	8%
Gender:		
Men	8%	12%
Women	6%	12%
Mass attendance:		
Weekly	8%	16%
Monthly	6%	14%
Yearly	6%	8%
Seldom/never	8%	13%
Ethnic group:		
Non-Hispanic	8%	13%
Hispanic	5%	9%
Region:		
Northwest	6%	10%
Midwest	10%	15%
South	9%	13%
West	5%	11%

TAKEN FROM: "Catholic Reactions to the Sex Abuse Scandal," *National Catholic Reporter*, October 28, 2011.

crimes against humanity—that these offenses have been committed, and are still being committed, on a widespread *and* systematic basis. Those crimes that occurred pre-2002 (the year the Statute of the International Criminal Court entered into force) are not simply "historical violations" that have no bearing on the post-2002 crimes or, indeed, the current policies and practices of the Vatican. The pre-2002 crimes, as well as post-2002 offenses, demonstrate: the widespread and systematic nature of the attack on children and vulnerable adults; that high-level Vatican officials, including Joseph Ratzinger, were on notice of the serious crisis facing the Catholic church in relation to sexual violence committed against children and vulnerable adults, the scope and scale of the crimes; and that the Vatican policy and practice was to protect the Church rather than protect the victims. Moreover, the pre-2002 cases establish many situations where the perpetrator has benefitted from the culture of impunity and may still be a danger to children and vulnerable adults, victims continue to suffer and the systemic culture of sexual violence continues. . . .

An Abundance of Evidence

The testimony, case studies, expert declarations, letters, statements, photographs, findings of multiple commissions of inquiry and grand juries, guilty pleas of bishops to charges like 'failing to report a crime', etc. [are] merely a sample or representation of the vast amount of information and documentation currently available. Even the currently available information is likely just the tip of an iceberg. It must be acknowledged that much of this evidence has come to light through the heroic efforts of survivors, supporters, whistleblowers, lawyers, investigators operating in different places at different times addressing specific situations in different contexts. Eventually, as a result of their efforts and courage, the picture has become clearer as common themes emerged and bishops and cardinals have run out of ways to explain away more and more instances of sexual violence the more the truth continued to slip through the grasp of those who would keep it hidden. . . .

For many, the fact that the Vatican has had a longstanding policy and practice for dealing with sexual violence by priests in ways that have ensured such violence would continue is as shocking as the magnitude and gravity of the offenses themselves. That church officials would place such little value on the children, vulnerable adults and communities they deliberately exposed and placed at risk will no doubt be difficult to comprehend. But the facts speak for themselves. And, the facts will show that, in effect, those with power in the Vatican have helped foster a culture of rape within the church—a culture that, when left to its own devices, accepts it, condones it and, ultimately, perpetuates it.

> "Men who target children are no more pervasive in the priesthood (and perhaps less pervasive) than in any other segment of society."

The Truth About Priests

Michael Friscolanti

In the following viewpoint, Maclean's senior writer Michael Friscolanti argues that the popular perception since the Catholic sex abuse scandal that all priests are pedophiles is not based in reality. In fact, he says, priests are no more likely to abuse children than are members of the general public. He points out that the majority of sexual abuse takes place in the home, and that other religious clergy may have the same rate of abuse as Catholic priests do, but only Catholic clergy are being targeted.

As you read, consider the following questions:

1. With what crime was Bishop Raymond Lahey charged, after announcing an out-of-court settlement for sex abuse victims in his diocese?

2. According to the author, who is to blame for the stereotype of pedophile priests?

Michael Friscolanti, "The Truth About Priests," *Maclean's*, December 1, 2009. Copyright © 2009 by Maclean's Magazine. All rights reserved. Republished with permission.

3. What percentage of the Chicago Archdiocese's priests were sexual abusers, according to its self-study?

Even to the eyes of a seasoned child pornography investigator, the photographs are horrific. One image depicts a young boy, no older than 12, standing on a wooden deck, a pair of white underwear pulled down around his knees. In the next shot, a different naked boy is sitting in an office chair, with two holy rosaries—one white, one black—dangling from his skinny neck. It's impossible to know for sure, but detectives believe the anonymous boy could be as young as nine years old.

In yet another photo—one of 964 discovered on Bishop Raymond Lahey's laptop—a male teenager is posing in front of a bookcase. "He is blond and looks hurt as there are red welts and marks on his stomach and chest area," according to a police statement filed in court. "He looks sad in this image."

Sadness does not even begin to describe such a betrayal. In August [2009], the same Bishop Lahey proudly announced a historic, out-of-court settlement worth millions of dollars for victims who were sexually assaulted by Catholic priests in his diocese of Antigonish, N.S. [Nova Scotia, Canada]. Then, just weeks after the press release, he was flagged by border guards following a flight from England to Ottawa, and—after a peek inside his Toshiba [laptop]—charged with possessing and importing child pornography.

Like everyone, Lahey is entitled to his day in court (his next appearance is Dec. 16 [2009]). As he told police during his first interrogation, he has "never done anything that would be abusive with a child" and has "no time for child exploitation." His downloads, however, tell a much more sinister story: when the good bishop wasn't negotiating with victims of sexual abuse, he was in his rectory, staring at graphic images of the very same crime.

Though shocking, Lahey's arrest was not exactly surprising. Sadly, he is just the latest in a long, infamous line of

Catholic clergymen accused of preying on innocent children (or in his case, watching from afar as others prey on innocent children). The headlines have been repeated so many times over so many years that it's difficult to look at any man in a Roman collar and not assume the worst. Of course Bishop Lahey had kiddie porn on his computer. All priests are pedophiles.

In pop culture, at least, that presumption is now gospel truth. *Doubt*, last year's [2008's] Oscar-winning movie, centres on a priest suspected of sexually abusing a student. The latest Scotiabank Giller Prize [Canada's most prestigious literary award] was awarded to Linden MacIntyre's *The Bishop's Man*, a novel that tells the story of a guilt-ridden East Coast cleric whose job is to clean up—and cover up—any whiff of scandal in the diocese. And if a priest shows up in an episode of *Law & Order*, odds are he is attracted to nine-year-old boys. "I've seen TV shows where the surprise ending is that the priest is not the pedophile," says Philip Jenkins, a professor at Penn State University and author of *Pedophiles and Priests: Anatomy of a Contemporary Crisis*.

The media is not to blame for the allegations against Bishop Lahey—or the sins of any other priest who uses his spiritual authority to violate a child. If parishioners assume the man saying mass is a molester, it's because thousands of priests actually were molesters. *Law & Order* did not invent the stereotype, and neither did newspapers. Priests did.

But at the risk of downplaying decades of unspeakable abuse—or forgiving a Church hierarchy that moved heaven and earth to suppress scandal and protect criminal clergy—an obvious point is often ignored: the vast, vast majority of Catholic priests are not sexual predators. In fact, the scientific research suggests that men who target children are no more pervasive in the priesthood (and perhaps less pervasive) than in any other segment of society. Depending on the study, somewhere between two and four per cent of priests have had

[The 2004 John Jay College report found] that *a little less than half of the priests [accused of sexual abuse] (1881) were found to be subject to unsubstantiated allegations.* An unsubstantiated allegation was defined as "an allegation that was proven to be untruthful and fabricated" as a result of a criminal investigation. This rate of false accusations is much higher than found in the general population. Additionally, 23% of the priests who were accused of abuse were identified as suffering from behavioral or psychological problems ranging from alcohol and substance abuse to depression and a past history of coercive sex, although most never received treatment for these problems.

William O'Donohue, Olga Cirlugea, and Lorraine Benuto, Catholic League for Religious and Civil Rights, April 27, 2012.

sexual contact with a minor. Or, to put it another way, between 96 and 98 per cent have not.

"It's part of that myth—the myth of the pedophile priest who can't help himself," says Thomas Plante, a psychology professor at Santa Clara University who has published dozens of studies about sexually abusive priests. "It's really an issue of perception rather than reality. Believe it or not, probably the safest place for a kid to be is in a Catholic church environment."

That certainly wasn't the case for John Swales and his two younger brothers, Guy and Ed. Back in the summer of 1969, the boys attended a summer camp for low-income kids where they met a charming, larger-than-life volunteer named Father Barry Glendinning. An instructor at St. Peter's Seminary in London, Ont. [Ontario, Canada], the priest soon became a surrogate big brother. He gained the trust of the boys' parents, showered them with pizzas, movies and booze, and, when opportunity knocked, introduced them to sex. John was 10 years old when the first assault took place. "You name it, he did it," Swales says.

Glendinning was later convicted of six counts of gross indecency, but for Swales, the damage was already done. His life spiralled into a hell of drug addiction and male prostitution. "I'm coming out on the other end, but there is no healing," he says now, 40 years later. "The impact is so intense and so deep-rooted it is beyond comprehension and beyond my ability to express it. That sounds melodramatic, but when you have sex at the age of 10 with your priest, it's pretty weird."

In 2004, the Swales family won a landmark $1.3-million judgment against Glendinning and the London diocese, but not before a bitter court battle that dragged on for years. The diocese went so far as to file a countersuit against John, claiming he was to blame for some of his brothers' pain because he also molested them—albeit after Glendinning molested all three of them. The judge was not convinced: "Blaming John for his assaults on his siblings would be similar to blaming Frankenstein's monster for his actions, rather than attributing its behaviour to the scientist who created it."

Tragically, the Swales saga is not an isolated one. The Catholic Church, both in Canada and abroad, is rife with stories of priests who took advantage of vulnerable kids—and bishops who, at the first sign of trouble, simply shuffled them off to a different parish. Kevin Bennett. Charles Sylvestre. Thomas O'Dell. Bernard Prince. John Geoghan. Mount Cashel Orphanage. The list goes on and on.

But as implausible as it may sound—especially so soon after Bishop Lahey's arrest—the Catholic priesthood is not overflowing with serial sex offenders. For all the pain he inflicted, Barry Glendinning is an exception, not the rule. "What has happened with some priests is obviously extremely distressing, but it is important to remember that this is still a very tiny percentage of priests that we're talking about," says Frederick

Berlin, founder of the sexual disorders clinic at Johns Hopkins Hospital in Baltimore. "It's important to put this into the proper context."

Context, of course, is often mistaken for a cop-out. But after so much scandal, knowing the stats is arguably just as important as knowing what Lahey was hiding on his laptop.

In 1993, experts analyzed the files of 1,322 priests who were hospitalized over a 25-year period at Southdown Institute, an Ontario facility that treats clergy suffering from a wide range of psychological disorders. Fewer than three per cent were pedophiles. Around the same time, the archdiocese of Chicago examined its own records over the previous 40 years—spanning more than 2,200 priests—and reopened every internal complaint. The result: fewer than two per cent sexually abused a child. A New York Times analysis conducted a decade later found the same rate across the United States: 1.8 per cent.

The bible of all such studies was released in 2004. Commissioned by American bishops and conducted by the John Jay College of Criminal Justice, the analysis was both startling and sobering: between 1950 and 2002, exactly 4,392 priests and deacons in the U.S.—four per cent—were accused of child sexual abuse. There were a total of 10,667 victims, and the allegations ranged from touching over clothing (52.6 per cent) to penile penetration (22.4 per cent).

The revelation that four out of every 100 priests were leading double lives is hardly reassuring. And one victim—let alone 10,667—is one victim too many. But if nothing else, the John Jay study does offer compelling proof that priests, on average, don't seem to be any more dangerous than the people sitting in their pews.

Nobody knows for sure how often Boy Scout leaders or hockey coaches or daycare workers abuse the children under their watch. Headlines are the only indication. But consider this stat: according to the most reliable figures, 13 per cent of men and up to 40 per cent of women say they were sexually abused as children. The huge majority of those crimes occur inside the home—and the culprit is usually a relative, not the local priest. "We don't know what the prevalence rate is for the general population, but it has to be at least double what it is for priests," Plante says. "We can estimate it backwards through the lens of the victim."

We also don't know the prevalence among other religious leaders. So while four per cent may seem high (or low), it's impossible to say whether rabbis or imams or pastors are violating children at the same pace as their Catholic counterparts. "It's clear that the Catholic Church has a bull's eye on it," says Leslie Lothstein, a Connecticut-based psychologist who has counselled hundreds of wayward clergy. "No one is really collecting that data systematically for all Protestant sects. The same is true for the Jewish clergy, and while little is known about the Muslim clergy, it's clear that when you actually work with people who are sexually abused, everyone seems to be part of the act."

> "Sexual assault is clearly an issue in need of attention by the campus community given its high prevalence and adverse consequences."

There Is a Serious Problem with Sexual Assault on College Campuses

Christopher P. Krebs et al.

The following viewpoint presents findings from a study on sexual assault on college campuses conducted by researchers Christopher P. Krebs and colleagues at the Research Triangle Institute with a grant from the US Department of Justice. The authors explain that sexual assault on campuses is prevalent, with victims being primarily women, and assailants generally being people they know and trust. Krebs et al. discuss the various types of such assaults, including use of drugs without the victims' knowledge, and victims' voluntary use of alcohol or other drugs, factors in the majority of assaults. Also noted is the significant underreporting of sexual assaults on campuses.

Christopher P. Krebs, Christine H. Lindquist, Tara D. Warner, Bonnie S. Fisher, and Sandra L. Martin, "Conclusions and Recommendations," *The Campus Sexual Assault Study*, December 2007, sec. 6, pp. 1–4.

As you read, consider the following questions:

1. What percentage of college women studied experienced sexual assault after voluntarily consuming alcohol or drugs, according to the authors?

2. At what point in a student's college career is she most likely to be sexually assaulted, according to Krebs et al.?

3. What racial differences in perpetrators of forced sexual assaults versus incapacitated assaults did the authors find?

It is quite clear that a sizeable proportion of undergraduate women (11.1%) have experienced sexual assault when they were incapacitated and unable to provide consent, but the large majority of these victims had not been given a drug without their knowledge prior to the assault. The large majority (566, 84%) of the 651 women who experienced incapacitated sexual assault were victims of AOD [alcohol and/or other drug]-enabled, rather than drug-facilitated, sexual assault [DFSA]. Only 31 (0.6%) of the 5,446 undergraduate women who participated in the CSA [campus sexual assault] Study reported being sexually assaulted after being given a drug without their knowledge or consent since entering college. There are no estimates in the literature to which this figure can be compared, but given the attention that DFSA and "date rape drugs" have received in the media in recent years, this estimate is almost certainly lower than some might have expected. Clearly, undergraduate women are at much greater risk of sexual assault that occurs in the context of voluntary consumption of alcohol and/or drugs or that is physically forced than sexual assault that is drug facilitated.

The phenomenon of being given a drug without one's knowledge is, however, not necessarily rare among our sample. A total of 308 women in our sample of 5,446 (5.3%) reported being given a drug without their knowledge or consent since entering college and the drugs most likely to be administered were Rohypnol and GHB [gamma-hydroxybutyric acid], which are commonly referred to as date rape drugs. Women being given a drug without their knowledge or consent appears [to] be a legitimate concern for universities and students, but it is unclear whether widespread concerns about DFSA can be justified empirically.

Who Are the Victims?

Another interesting finding generated by the CSA Study is that the prevalence of experiencing sexual assault is higher since entering college (13.7%) than before entering college (11.3%). However, our survey was done at a single point in time and during a time period when collegiate experiences are more salient, so it may be that subjects had difficulty recalling sexual assaults that occurred before entering college. On the other hand, it is important to point out that our "since entering college" estimates do not reflect the sample's entire collegiate experience because the sample includes freshman, sophomores, and juniors (and even seniors had not completed their senior year), which means that the true rate of sexual assault during the entire college experience is likely higher. When subsetting to seniors, the data show that 368 women (26.1% of seniors) reported experiencing attempted or completed sexual assault since entering college. Ninety-two (7.0%) seniors were victims of physically forced sexual assault since entering college, and 223 (16.0%) seniors were victims of incapacitated sexual assault since entering college. It is important to note, however, that although the cumulative prevalence estimates of sexual assault are understandably highest for seniors, the "past 12 month" prevalence estimates of sexual assault are highest among sophomores. This pattern indicates that women who are victimized during college are most likely to be victimized early on in their college tenure. This finding is consistent with a [2006] study employing a convenience sample of university women, which found that 84% of the women who reported sexually coercive situations experienced the incident during their first four semesters on campus.

Not surprisingly, the CSA Study found that the prevalence of sexual assault among male college students was considerably lower than similar estimates for women. A total of 50 males (3.7%) reported being victims of completed sexual assault since entering college. The majority of these victims (90.2%) were victims of incapacitated sexual assault. Estimates of the sexual victimization of adult males are sparse in the literature, so it is difficult to compare the CSA Study findings to those produced by existing research.

Different Risk Factors

Our ... analyses identifying risk factors for sexual assault among university women indicate that several factors are differentially associated with specific types of sexual assault. Specifically, compared to whites, Hispanic women were more likely to be victims of physically forced sexual assault. Years in college and the number of dating partners were both positively associated with experiencing physically forced sexual assault and experiencing physically forced and AOD-enabled sexual assault. Victims of AOD-enabled assault and both types of assault more frequently attended fraternity parties, got drunk, had ever been given a drug without their consent, and were frequently drunk during sex since entering college. Victims of AOD-enabled sexual assault only were more likely to have used marijuana. In contrast, none of these risk factors were significantly associated with being a victim of forced sexual assault. Ever having been threatened, humiliated, or physically hurt by a dating partner was a risk factor for all three measures of sexual assault. Interestingly, having been a victim of forced sexual assault before entering college was a risk factor for being a victim of forced (but not AOD-enabled) sexual assault since entering college, and having been a victim

Campus Rape Is a Public Health Crisis

Rape on campus is a very real problem. Cautious estimates suggest that nearly one in every 10 female college students will be raped while she's at school. With an estimated 18 million students attending college in the U.S. this year, that's (conservatively) over 130,000 young women who'll be raped while at college this year alone. That's a public health crisis. It's time to start treating it like one.

Jaclyn Friedman, American Prospect, *September 8, 2009.*

of incapacitated sexual assault before entering college was a risk factor for being a victim of AOD-enabled (but not forced) sexual assault since entering college. Other studies have found that previous victimization is a risk factor for future victimization, but this is the first study we are aware of that has determined that being a victim of a certain type of sexual assault puts one at risk of being a victim of that type of sexual assault, and not necessarily another type of sexual assault. In other words, the risk posed by previous victimization is specific to the type of victimization experienced.

Forced vs. Incapacitated Assault

Descriptive analyses of the context, consequences, and reporting of sexual assault also confirm that differences exist between forced and incapacitated sexual assault. For example, forced sexual assaults were more likely to involve a black perpetrator, whereas incapacitated sexual assaults were more likely to involve a white perpetrator. Forced assaults were also more likely to be perpetrated by a stranger to the victim or an exdating partner or ex-spouse, whereas incapacitated sexual assaults were more likely to be perpetrated by a friend or acquaintance of the victim. Additionally, more than a quarter of incapacitated sexual assault victims were victimized by a member of a fraternity. Not surprisingly, victims of incapacitated sexual assault were considerably more likely to have been using alcohol before and be drunk during the assault. Incapacitated assaults were more likely to happen at a party and between midnight and 6 a.m., whereas forced sexual assaults were more likely to happen between noon and midnight. Victims of forced sexual assault were more likely to be injured and to consider the incident to be rape.

Victims of forced sexual assault were more likely to report the assault to friends or family, crisis centers, and law enforcement, but they were also less satisfied with how the report was handled and more likely to regret reporting the assault than incapacitated sexual assault victims who reported their assaults. Overall, victims of forced sexual assault were also more likely to make changes in their lives in reaction to the assault, such as dropping a class, moving, and changing majors, and were more likely to seek psychological counseling as a result of the victimization.

Study Results Carry Implications

Sexual assault is clearly an issue in need of attention by the campus community given its high prevalence and adverse consequences, and the CSA Study results carry many social and policy-oriented implications. One out of five undergraduate women experience an attempted or completed sexual assault since entering college. Moreover, attention must be paid to the following facts:

- the majority of sexual assaults occur when women are incapacitated due to their use of substances, primarily alcohol;

- freshmen and sophomores are at greater risk for victimization than juniors and seniors; and

- the large majority of victims of sexual assault are victimized by men they know and trust, rather than strangers.

It is thus critical that sexual assault prevention strategies and messages be designed such that undergraduates are educated (and as soon after enrollment as possible) about these facts. Most importantly, because most sexual assaults experienced by university women are enabled by alcohol or other drugs, one clear implication is the need to address the risks of substance use, particularly the risk of drinking to excess, in sexual assault prevention messages presented to university students. For many students, college offers an environment notorious for encouraging excessive drinking and experimenting with drugs. Most students are simply unable to gauge the amount of alcohol consumed, are unaware of the effects of new drugs or the mixing of drugs and alcohol, and are unfamiliar with the point at which their cognitive ability is so impaired that they cannot protect themselves. Students may also be unaware of the image of vulnerability projected by a visibly intoxicated individual. Despite the link between substance use and sexual assault, it appears that few sexual assault prevention and/or risk reduction programs address the relationship between substance use and sexual assault. In a review of 15 university-based prevention interventions conducted between 1994 and 1999, only three included references to alcohol use.

Another Important Implication

Another important implication stems from our finding of DFSA being an extremely rare occurrence. Universities should continue to be mindful of this phenomenon and educate students about the potential dangers and consequences of clandestinely giving someone a drug or being given a drug. However, an overemphasis on DFSA takes attention away from the true nature of campus sexual assault, ignoring the fact that most sexual assaults occur after voluntary alcohol consumption by the victim and assailant. Universities must address the dangers of voluntary alcohol consumption rather than focusing on the rare phenomenon of coercive drug ingestion.

Finally, the very low rates of reporting sexual assault to crisis centers and law enforcement suggest that perhaps more can be done to encourage reporting. When reports of sexual assault are handled properly and effectively, the process can be important to the recovery and healing of the victim, as well as the identification, punishment, and deterrence of perpetration. Universities and law enforcement should thus seek out and implement strategies that encourage reporting of sexual assault and ensure reports of sexual assault are being handled properly. The fact that a large proportion of sexual assault victims had been drinking before the incident may particularly discourage reporting, given victim concerns about reprisal for violating campus policies on drug and alcohol use. Other studies have suggested that university administrators believe policies allowing for confidential and anonymous reporting encourage reporting.

In addition, even though some women experience their first sexual assault after entering college, many women who experience sexual assault during college had been sexually victimized before coming to college. Since women who have experienced sexual assault before entering college have a much greater chance of experiencing sexual assault during college, it is important that sexual assault programming reflects this reality. Programs should focus on both primary prevention for women who have not experienced sexual assault and secondary prevention in an effort to prevent re-victimization.

| "*Most campus 'rape' cases exist in the gray area of seeming cooperation and tacit consent.*"

College Campus Rape Statistics Are Exaggerated

Heather Mac Donald

In the following viewpoint, writer Heather Mac Donald, a John M. Olin Fellow at the Manhattan Institute and a contributing editor of City Journal, *challenges claims that sexual assault on college campuses is a serious problem. She argues that the numbers behind this allegation are the result of flawed research methods that actually seek to inflate sexual assault rates to fuel what Mac Donald calls the "campus rape industry." Many so-called rapes, she says, are the products of "hookup culture" and not even considered rape by the alleged victims.*

As you read, consider the following questions:

1. According to the campus sexual-assault organizations Mac Donald refers to, what percentage of college women are victims of rape or attempted rape?

Heather Mac Donald, "What Campus Rape Crisis?," *Los Angeles Times*, February 24, 2008. Copyright © 2008 Heather Mac Donald. All rights reserved. Republished with permission.

2. What was the problem with Mary Koss's method of questioning female students, in the author's view?

3. How many sexual assaults are commonly reported on college campuses, according to Mac Donald?

It's a lonely job, working the phones at a college rape crisis center. Day after day, you wait for the casualties to show up from the alleged campus rape epidemic—but no one calls. Could this mean that the crisis is overblown? No. It means, according to campus sexual-assault organizations, that the abuse of coeds is worse than anyone had ever imagined. It means that consultants and counselors need more funding to persuade student rape victims to break the silence of their suffering.

It is a central claim of these organizations that between a fifth and a quarter of all college women will be raped or will be the targets of attempted rape by the end of their college years. Harvard's Office of Sexual Assault Prevention and Response uses the 20% to 25% statistic. Websites at New York University, Syracuse University, Penn State and the University of Virginia, among many other places, use the figures as well.

And who will be the assailants of these women? Not terrifying strangers who will grab them in dark alleys, but the guys sitting next to them in class or at the cafeteria.

No Such Crisis

If the one-in-four statistic is correct, campus rape represents a crime wave of unprecedented proportions. No felony, much less one as serious as rape, has a victimization rate remotely approaching 20% or 25%, even over many years. The 2006 violent crime rate in Detroit, one of the most violent cities in the U.S., was 2,400 murders, rapes, robberies, and aggravated assaults per 100,000 inhabitants—a rate of 2.4%.

Such a crime wave—in which millions of young women would graduate having suffered the most terrifying assault,

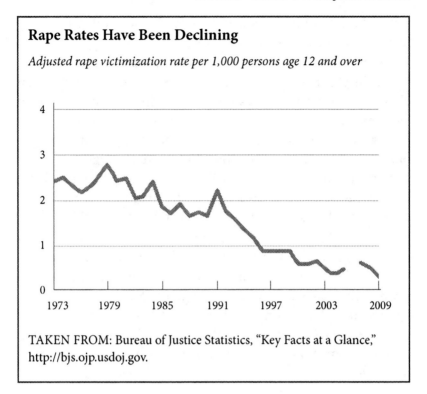

Rape Rates Have Been Declining

Adjusted rape victimization rate per 1,000 persons age 12 and over

TAKEN FROM: Bureau of Justice Statistics, "Key Facts at a Glance," http://bjs.ojp.usdoj.gov.

short of murder, that a woman can experience—would require nothing less than a state of emergency. Admissions policies, which if the numbers are true are allowing in tens of thousands of vicious criminals, would require a complete revision, perhaps banning male students entirely. The nation's nearly 10 million female undergraduates would need to take the most stringent safety precautions.

None of this crisis response occurs, of course—because the [campus sexual assault] crisis doesn't exist.

A Flawed Study

So where do the numbers come from? During the 1980s, feminist researchers committed to the rape-culture theory discovered that asking women directly if they had been raped yielded disappointing results—very few women said that they had been. So *Ms.* magazine commissioned University of Arizona public health professor Mary Koss to develop a different way to measure the prevalence of rape.

Rather than asking female students about rape per se, Koss asked them if they had ever experienced actions that she then classified as rape. One question, for example, asked, "Have you had sexual intercourse when you didn't want to because a man gave you alcohol or drugs?"—a question that is ambiguous on several fronts, including the woman's degree of incapacitation, the causal relation between being given a drink and having sexual intercourse, and the man's intentions. Koss' method produced the 25% rate, which *Ms.* then published.

It was a flawed study on a number of levels, but the most powerful refutation came from her own subjects: 73% of the women whom the study characterized as rape victims told the researchers that they hadn't been raped. Further, 42% of the study's supposed victims said they had had intercourse again with their alleged assailants—though it is highly unlikely that a raped woman would have sex again with the fiend who attacked her.

Victims' Interpretations Ignored

Despite all this, the numbers have stuck. Today, John Foubert, an education professor at William and Mary College (and founder of a group called One-in-Four, which works on sexual assault issues and has chapters on 17 campuses), says, "The one-in-four statistic has been replicated in several studies for several decades. To the extent that social science can prove anything, which I believe it can, the one-in-four statistic has been proven beyond all reasonable doubt. My instincts tell me that the statistic is actually much higher."

Yet subsequent campus rape studies keep turning up the pesky divergence between the victims' and the researchers' point of view.

A 2006 survey of sorority women at the University of Virginia, for example, found that only 23% of the subjects whom the survey characterized as rape victims felt that they had been raped—a result that the university's director of sexual and domestic violence services calls "discouraging." Equally damning was a 2000 campus rape study conducted under the aegis of the Department of Justice. Sixty-five percent of those whom the researchers called "completed rape" victims and three-quarters of "attempted rape" victims said that they did not think that their experiences were "serious enough to report."

Believing in the campus rape epidemic, it turns out, requires ignoring women's own interpretations of their experiences.

Ubiquitous but Underused Facilities

Nevertheless, none of the weaknesses in the research has had the slightest drag on the campus "anti-rape" movement, because the movement is political, not empirical. In a rape culture, which "condones physical and emotional terrorism against women as a norm," sexual assault will wind up underreported, argued Carole Goldberg, the director of Yale's Sexual Harassment and Assault Resources and Education Center, in a March 2007 newsletter. Campus rape centers and 24-hour hotlines, aided by tens of millions of dollars of federal funding, are ubiquitous.

Needless to say, those facilities don't appear to get a tremendous amount of use. For example, Hillary Wing-Richards, the associate director of sexual-assault prevention at James Madison University, said the school's campus rape "help line" gets a varying number of calls, some of which are "request-for-information calls"—where to go, who to talk to and the like.

"Some months there are 10 and others, one or two," she said.

Referring to rape hotlines, risk management consultant Brett Sokolow laments: "The problem is, on so many of our campuses, very few people ever call. And mostly we've resigned ourselves to the underutilization of these resources."

Federal law requires colleges to publish reported crimes affecting their students. The numbers of reported sexual assaults—the law does not require their confirmation—usually run under half a dozen a year on private campuses, and maybe two to three times that at large public universities.

A New Gray Area

So what reality does lie behind the rape hype? I believe that it's the booze-fueled hookup culture of one-night, or sometimes just partial-night, stands. Students in the '60s demanded that college administrators stop setting rules for fraternization. The colleges meekly complied and opened a Pandora's box of boorish, promiscuous behavior that gets cruder each year.

This culture has been written about widely. College women—as well as men—reportedly drink heavily before and during parties. For the women, that drinking is often goal-oriented, suggests Karin Agness, a recent University of Virginia graduate and founder of NeW, a club for conservative university women: It frees the drinker from responsibility and "provides an excuse for engaging in behavior that she ordinarily wouldn't." Nights can include a meaningless sexual encounter with a guy whom the girl may not even know.

In all these drunken couplings, there may be some deplorable instances of forced and truly non-consensual sex. But most campus "rape" cases exist in the gray area of seeming cooperation and tacit consent, which is why they are almost never prosecuted criminally.

"Ninety-nine percent of all college rape cases would be thrown out of court in a twinkling," observes University of Pennsylvania history professor Alan Kors.

Female Students Share Responsibility

Many students hold on to the view that women usually have the power to determine whether a campus social event ends with intercourse. A female Rutgers student expressed a common sentiment in a university sexual-assault survey: "When we go out to parties and I see girls and the way they dress and the way they act ... and just the way they are, under the influence and um, then they like accuse them of like, 'Oh yeah, my boyfriend did this to me' or whatever, I honestly always think it's their fault."

But suggest to a rape bureaucrat that female students share responsibility for the outcome of an evening and that greater sexual restraint would prevent campus "rape," and you might as well be saying that women should don the burka [the full-body garment worn in public by Muslim women].

College officials have responded to the fallout of the college sexual revolution not with sound advice but with bizarre and anachronistic legalisms for responding to postcoital second thoughts.

University of Virginia students, for example, may demand a formal adjudication before the Sexual Assault Board; they can request a "structured meeting" with the Office of the Dean of Students by filing a formal complaint; or they can seek voluntary mediation.

Risk-management consultants travel the country to help colleges craft legal rules for student sexual congress.

"If one partner puts a condom on the other, does that signify that they are consenting to intercourse?" asks Alan D. Berkowitz, a campus rape consultant. Short of guiding the thus-sheathed instrumentality to port, it's hard to imagine a clearer signal of consent, although Berkowitz apparently finds it "inherently ambiguous."

Colleges Send Mixed Messages

And even as the campus rape industry decries alleged male predation, a parallel campus sex bureaucracy sends the message that students should have recreational sex at every opportunity.

New York University offers workshops on orgasms and "Sex Toys for Safer Sex" ("an evening with rubber, silicone and vibrating toys") in residence halls and various student clubs. Brown University's Student Services helps students answer the compelling question: "How can I bring sex toys into my relationship?" Princeton University's "Safer Sex Jeopardy" game for freshmen lists six types of vibrators and eight kinds of penile toys.

Why, exactly, are schools offering workshops on orgasms? Are students already so saturated with knowledge of the evolution of constitutional democracy, say, that colleges should reroute their resources to matters available on porn websites?

Remarkably, many students emerge from this farrago [confused mixture] of mixed messages with common sense intact.

In a November column in the University of Virginia's student newspaper, a third-year student gave the real scoop on frat parties: They're filled with men hoping to have sex. Rather than calling these men "rapists," columnist Katelyn Kiley offered some practical wisdom to the women trooping off to Virginia's fraternity row:

"It's probably a good idea to keep your clothes on, and at the end of the night, to go home to your own bed. Interestingly enough, that's how you get [the guys] to keep asking you back."

Maybe such young iconoclasts can take up another discredited idea: College is for learning. Fighting male dominance or catering to the libidinal impulses released in the 1960s are sorry substitutes for the pursuit of knowledge.

I *"Sexual assault within the military is a severe and pervasive problem."*

Sexual Assault in the US Military: A Review of the Literature and Recommendations for the Future

Jessica A. Turchik and Susan M. Wilson

Jessica A. Turchik is a postdoctoral research fellow in psychiatry and behavioral science at Stanford University. Susan M. Wilson is a doctoral student in psychology at Ohio University. In the following viewpoint, they examine the wealth of research conducted on the problem of sexual assault within the military. According to most data, they say, rates of sexual assault of both men and women in the military are as high or higher than those in civilian life, even before taking into account the small portion of a lifetime generally spent in military service.

Jessica A. Turchik and Susan M. Wilson, "Sexual Assault in the US Military: A Review of the Literature and Recommendations for the Future," *Aggression and Violent Behavior*, vol. 15, no. 4, July–August 2010, pp. 267–77. Copyright © 2010 by Elsevier. All rights reserved. Republished with permission.

As you read, consider the following questions:

1. According to studies mentioned by the authors, what is the range of rates for sexual assaults reported by males in the military?

2. What change do Turchik and Wilson say accounts for the increase in rates of sexual assaults in the military from 2004 to 2005 and 2005 to 2006?

3. Which branch of the military had the highest number of sexual assaults reported in 2007, according to the authors?

Sexual violence is an endemic problem in our society, as evidenced by the fact that approximately 18% to 25% of American women report experiencing either an attempted or completed rape in their lifetimes. A [2007] national study reported that 11% of U.S. women reported an incident of completed rape in their lifetime. Among men, approximately 3% to 4% of American men report an attempted or completed rape during adulthood. The reported rates of sexual assault in the military are as high or higher than those reported by civilians, but taking into account that the rates only include sexual assaults that took place during one's military service, the rates are very high. There are also fewer studies of MSA [military sexual assault] than general sexual assault among civilian samples. And many of the studies of MSA have methodological issues that future research will hopefully address.

Between 9.5% and 33% of women report experiencing an attempted or completed rape while serving in the military. A large scale study of active-duty Air Force women found that 9.5% of women reported that their most recent rape experience occurred while serving in the military, while another study of active-duty servicemembers across branches (Army heavily represented) found that 10.5% of women reported an attempted or completed rape. A number of studies of female veterans have assessed for sexual victimization during military service: [A 1996 study] found that 19.6% of women who sought services at one Veterans Affairs (VA) medical center reported an instance of rape. [A study in 2000] found that among a group of veterans who served after the Vietnam era 11% reported an attempted rape and 19% a completed rape; [another] found that among a nationwide sample utilizing VA health services 23% of women reported that "someone had used force or the threat of force to have sexual relations with them against their will." [In 1998, researchers] found that 43% of women utilizing VA services for stress disorders reported an instance of attempted or completed rape; and [a study in 2007] found that 33% of those who utilized VA medical or counseling services experienced an instance of unwanted oral, anal, or vaginal sex. If one includes sexual harassment and other forms of sexual assault, the rates reported during military service by women range from 22% to 84%.

A few studies have gathered prevalence rates on male victims in the military with rates of reported sexual assault ranging from 1% to 12%. However, it is not clear from many of the studies with male victims whether these sexual assaults occurred during military service. For example, [in 1999, researchers] reported a lifetime prevalence of sexual assault of 12% among 129 combat veterans consecutively referred for PTSD [post-traumatic stress disorder]. However, 92% of these assaults occurred prior to combat exposure, so it remains unclear whether these assaults actually occurred during or before military service. Similarly, in a group of Vietnam era veterans 11.8% reported some form of adult sexual abuse, but rates were not specifically reported for in-service assaults only. [A 1998 study] found that 6.7% of active-duty male Army soldiers had experienced sexual assault during their lifetimes and approximately 3% since entering the military.

In a large nationwide sample of veterans who used VA health services in 2003, 1% of men reported military sexual

Military Sexual Assault in the War on Terror

According to the Department of Defense [DoD] Report on Sexual Assault in the Military, there were 2,516 unrestricted reports and 714 restricted reports of servicemember-related sexual assaults in fiscal year 2009. This represents an overall increase of 11 percent from fiscal year 2008 and includes 1,338 servicemember-on-servicemember assaults and 215 assaults in Iraq and Afghanistan. These numbers do not reflect unreported assaults, and experts believe that the majority of victims, both civilian and military, never report their attacks, while the DoD report said only 20 percent of unwanted sexual contacts are reported to a military authority.

Elizabeth M. Collins,
Soldiers Magazine, *September 2010.*

trauma, while another small sample of veterans found that 4% of those seeking PTSD disability benefits reported an in-service sexual assault. A study of active-duty servicemembers (largely Army) found that 1.2% of men reported an attempted or completed rape. Reported rates of sexual harassment among men while in the military range from 36% to 74%, although men are less likely to acknowledge these types of behaviors as being sexual harassment compared to women.

As noted by [researchers in 2007], there is little consistency in the methodology, sample, definitions of sexual assault, and surveys or questions used to measure MSA, which likely accounts for the wide variation in prevalence rates across studies. Although methodological issues exist in many sexual assault studies regardless of the setting and sample, there are fewer studies that focus specifically on the military than college or community samples, the population is one that researchers have a more difficult time accessing, there is less consistency in MSA measures, and MSA studies are less often prospective. Studies of MSA are also often retrospective (sometimes asking participants about experiences that occurred over 20 years ago), are not Department of Defense (DoD) or servicewide, and do not break down sexual assault rates by service, war era, or other characteristics.

The majority of prevalence data comes from examining women as MSA victims. Fewer studies have examined male victims, and the vast majority of research assumes that the perpetrators are men and do not provide sex data on perpetrators. One report by the DoD noted that among the reported sexual assault cases in 2002 and 2003, 99% of alleged military offenders were male and 91% of the alleged victims were female. Therefore the focus of this [viewpoint] will be on female victims and male perpetrators, but other research will be discussed when it is available. It is important to note that although women are more likely to experience sexual assault than men and men are the vast majority of perpetrators, given the greater number of men in the military, the total number of male and female victims is approximately equal according to a recent nationwide sample of veterans.

Data also suggest that the reported rates of sexual assault have increased over time, with one study finding that 26.6% of female veterans who served before 1974 reported sexual assault, 32.9% who served between 1974 and 1981, and 32.4% who served after 1981. A 2002 DoD report, however, found that the reported rates of attempted and completed rape by women declined from 6% in 1995 to 3% in 2002. More recent [2006 and 2007] servicewide rates show increases from 2004 to 2005 and from 2005 to 2006, which are largely attributed to a restricted reporting system which began in June 2005. Some studies have not found differing rates of sexual assault among any of the five service branches. However, one study of sexual harassment found the highest rates in the Marine Corps and the lowest in the Air Force.

In 2007, the Army had more sexual assaults reported than any of the other three DoD branches (Marines, Air Force, and Navy) combined and the highest rate when the number of active-duty personnel in each service was taken into account. It is possible that these higher reporting rates may indicate a greater propensity to report rather than a greater incidence of sexual assault. However, it should be noted that the rates of sexual assault based on actual reports made while in the military (such as those typically reported by the DoD, service branches, and General Accountability Office reports) are thought to be an underestimate of the actual occurrence of sexual assault in the military, a trend that is consistent across both college and community samples of sexual assault research as well. Despite the variability of methodology across prevalence studies, it remains clear that sexual assault within the military is a severe and pervasive problem. More comprehensive and methodologically-sound research is needed to get a better sense of the true rates and characteristics of sexual assault in the military.

> *"Saint Augustine called rape 'an ancient and customary evil.' It has long been considered one of the spoils of war."*

War's Overlooked Victims

The Economist

The Economist *is a weekly newspaper focusing on international politics and business news and opinion. In the following viewpoint, the author discusses the history of rape as a war tactic and the public perception of this tactic. Rape was used on a mass scale in conflicts in Bosnia, Congo, Rwanda, and other war-torn areas, as a means of subjugating and destroying bonds between enemies and civilians. In more recent years, rape during war is reported and prosecuted more frequently, but still, many of the countries where it is used most pervasively are those with the least-reliable justice systems.*

As you read, consider the following questions:

1. When did the United Nations Security Council officially recognize rape as a war crime, according to the author?

2. According to the author, in which country's civil war was rape only rarely used?

3. How many prosecutions of rape as a war crime or crime against humanity have there been in Congo, according to *The Economist*?

"War's Overlooked Victims," *The Economist*, January 13, 2011. Copyright © 2011 by The Economist. All rights reserved. Republished with permission.

Shortly after the birth of her sixth child, Mathilde went with her baby into the fields to collect the harvest. She saw two men approaching, wearing what she says was the uniform of the FDLR, a Rwandan militia. Fleeing them she ran into another man, who beat her head with a metal bar. She fell to the ground with her baby and lay still. Perhaps thinking he had murdered her, the man went away. The other two came and raped her, then they left her for dead.

Mathilde's story is all too common. Rape in war is as old as war itself. After the sack of Rome 16 centuries ago Saint Augustine called rape in wartime an "ancient and customary evil". For soldiers, it has long been considered one of the spoils of war. Antony Beevor, a historian who has written about rape during the Soviet conquest of Germany in 1945, says that rape has occurred in war since ancient times, often perpetrated by undisciplined soldiers. But he argues that there are also examples in history of rape being used strategically, to humiliate and to terrorise, such as the Moroccan *regulares* in Spain's civil war.

As the reporting of rape has improved, the scale of the crime has become more horrifyingly apparent. And with the Bosnian war of the 1990s came the widespread recognition that rape has been used systematically as a weapon of war and that it must be punished as an egregious crime. In 2008 the UN Security Council officially acknowledged that rape has been used as a tool of war. With these kinds of resolutions and global campaigns against rape in war, the world has become more sensitive. At least in theory, the Geneva Conventions, governing the treatment of civilians in war, are respected by politicians and generals in most decent states. Generals from rich countries know that their treatment of civilians in the theatre of war comes under ever closer scrutiny. The laws and customs of war are clear. But in many parts of the world, in the Hobbesian anarchy of irregular war, with ill-disciplined private armies or militias, these norms carry little weight.

Take Congo; it highlights both how horribly common rape is, and how hard it is to document and measure, let alone stop. The eastern part of the country has been a seething mess since the Rwandan genocide of 1994. In 2008 the International Rescue Committee (IRC), a humanitarian group, estimated that 5.4m people had died in "Africa's world war". Despite peace deals in 2003 and 2008, the tempest of violence has yet fully to subside. As Congo's army and myriad militias do battle, the civilians suffer most. Rape has become an ugly and defining feature of the conflict.

Plenty of figures on how many women have been raped are available but none is conclusive. In October Roger Meece, the head of the United Nations in Congo, told the UN Security Council that 15,000 women had been raped throughout the country in 2009 (men suffer too, but most victims are female). The UN Population Fund estimated 17,500 victims for the same period. The IRC says it treated 40,000 survivors in the eastern province of South Kivu alone between 2003 and 2008.

"The data only tell you so much," says Hillary Margolis, who runs the IRC's sexual-violence programme in North Kivu. These numbers are the bare minimum; the true figures may be much higher. Sofia Candeias, who co-ordinates the UN Development Programme's Access to Justice project in Congo, points out that more rapes are reported in places with health services. In the areas where fighting is fiercest, women may have to walk hundreds of miles to find anyone to tell that they have been attacked. Even if they can do so, it may be months or years after the assault. Many victims are killed by their assailants. Others die of injuries. Many do not report rape because of the stigma.

Congo's horrors are mind-boggling. A recent study by the Harvard Humanitarian Initiative and Oxfam examined rape survivors at the Panzi Hospital in Bukavu, a town in South Kivu province. Their ages ranged from three to 80. Some were

single, some married, some widows. They came from all eth-
nicities. They were raped in homes, fields and forests. They
were raped in front of husbands and children. Almost 60%
were gang-raped. Sons were forced to rape mothers, and killed
if they refused.

The attention paid to Congo reflects growing concern
about rape in war. Historically the taboo surrounding rape
has been so strong that few cases were reported; evidence of
wartime rape before the 20th century is scarce. With better reporting, the world has woken up to the scale of the crime.
The range of sexual violence in war has become apparent: the
abduction of women as sex slaves, sexualised torture and mu-
tilation, rape in public or private.

In some wars all parties engage in it. In others it is inflicted mainly by one side. Rape in wars in Africa has had a
lot of attention in recent years, but it is not just an African
problem. Conflicts with high levels of rape between 1980 and
2009 were most numerous in sub-Saharan Africa, according to
Dara Kay Cohen of the University of Minnesota. But only a
third of sub-Saharan Africa's 28 civil wars saw the worst levels
of rape—compared with half of Eastern Europe's nine. And
no part of the world has escaped the scourge.

The anarchy and impunity of war goes some way to ex-
plaining the violence. The conditions of war are often condu-
cive to rape.

Young, ill-trained men, fighting far from home, are freed
from social and religious constraints. The costs of rape are
lower, the potential rewards higher. And for ill-fed, underpaid
combatants, rape can be a kind of payment.

Widespread, but not inevitable

Then consider the type of wars fought today. Many recent
conflicts have involved not organised armies but scrappy militias fighting amid civilians. As wars have moved from battle-

Customary Evil: Rape During Armed Conflicts

Conflict	Estimated number of rapes
Second Sino-Japanese War, Nanking, 1937	20,000 (Some 200,000 sex slaves were then provided for the Japanese army during World War II)
Soviet army in Germany, World War II	100,000–2,000,000
Pakistani army during the Bangladesh war of secession, 1971	200,000
Bosnian war, 1992–1995	20,000
Sierra Leone civil war, 1991–2002	More than 50,000
Rwandan genocide, 1994	500,000

TAKEN FROM: "War's Overlooked Victims," *The Economist*, January 13, 2011.

fields to villages, women and girls have become more vulnerable. For many, the home front no longer exists; every house is now on the front line.

But rape in war is not inevitable. In El Salvador's civil war, it was rare. When it did occur it was almost always carried out by state forces. The left-wing militias fighting against the government for years relied on civilians for information. You can rape to terrorise people or force them to leave an area, says Elisabeth Wood, a professor at Yale University and the Santa Fe Institute, but rape is not effective when you want long-term, reliable intelligence from them or to rule them in the future.

Some groups commit all kinds of other atrocities, but abhor rape. The absence of sexual violence in the Tamil Tigers' forced displacement of tens of thousands of Muslims from the

Jaffna peninsula in 1990 is a case in point. Rape is often part of ethnic cleansing but it was strikingly absent here. Tamil mores prohibit sex between people who are not married and sex across castes (though they are less bothered about marital rape). What is more, Ms. Wood explains, the organisation's strict internal discipline meant commanders could enforce these judgments.

Some leaders, such as Jean-Pierre Bemba, a Congolese militia boss who is now on trial for war-crimes in The Hague, say they lack full control over their troops. But a commander with enough control to direct soldiers in military operations can probably stop them raping, says Ms. Wood. A decision to turn a blind eye may have less to do with lack of control, and more with a chilling assessment of rape's use as a terror tactic.

Rape is a means of subduing foes and civilians without having to engage in the risky business of battle. Faced with rape, civilians flee, leaving their land and property to their attackers. In August rebel militias raped around 240 people over four days in the Walikale district of eastern Congo. The motives for the attack are unclear. The violence may have been to intimidate the population into providing the militia with gold and tin from nearby mines. Or maybe one bit of the army was colluding with the rebels to avoid being replaced by another bit and losing control of the area and its resources. In Walikale, at least, rape seems to have been a deliberate tactic, not a random one, says Ms. Margolis.

At worst, rape is a tool of ethnic cleansing and genocide, as in Bosnia, Darfur and Rwanda. Rape was first properly recognised as a weapon of war after the conflict in Bosnia. Though all sides were guilty, most victims were Bosnian Muslims assaulted by Serbs. Muslim women were herded into "rape camps" where they were raped repeatedly, usually by groups of men. The full horrors of these camps emerged in hearings at the war-crimes tribunal on ex-Yugoslavia in The Hague; victims gave evidence in writing or anonymously. After the war some perpetrators said that they had been ordered to rape—either to ensure that non-Serbs would flee certain areas, or to impregnate women so that they bore Serb children. In 1995, when Croatian forces overran Serb-held areas, there were well-attested cases of sexual violence against both women and men.

In the Sudanese region of Darfur, rape and other forms of sexual violence have also been a brutally effective way to terrorise and control civilians. Women are raped in and around the refugee camps that litter the region, mostly when they leave the camps to collect firewood, water and food. Those of the same ethnicity as the two main rebel groups have been targeted most as part of the campaign of ethnic cleansing. According to Human Rights Watch, rape is chronically underreported, partially because in the mostly Muslim region sexual violence is a sensitive subject. Between October 2004 and February 2005 Médecins Sans Frontières, a French charity, treated almost 500 women and girls in South Darfur. The actual number of victims is likely to be much higher.

Tacit approval

In the Rwandan genocide, rape was "the rule and its absence the exception", in the words of the UN. In the weeks before the killings began, Hutu-controlled newspapers ran cartoons showing Tutsi women having sex with Belgian peacekeepers, who were seen as allies of Paul Kagame's Rwandan Patriotic Front. Inger Skjelsbæk, deputy director of the Peace Research Institute in Oslo, argues that Hutu propaganda may not have openly called for rape, but it certainly suggested that the Hutu cause would be well served by the sexual violation of Tutsi women. Jens Meierhenrich, a Rwanda-watcher at the London School of Economics, says that even if high-level commanders did not tell men to rape, they gave tacit approval. Lower-ranking officers may have openly encouraged the crime.

Out of Rwanda's horror came the first legal verdict that acknowledged rape as part of a genocidal campaign. After the conviction of Jean Paul Akayesu, a local politician, the International Criminal Tribunal for Rwanda said systematic sexual violence, perpetrated against Tutsi women and them alone, had been an integral part of the effort to wipe out the Tutsis.

For combatants who know little about each other, complicity in rape can serve as a bond. The Revolutionary United Front (RUF) in Sierra Leone, most of whose members say they were kidnapped into its ranks and then raped thousands during the civil war, is a case in point. Ms. Cohen argues that armed groups that are not socially cohesive, particularly those whose fighters have been forcibly recruited, are more likely to commit rape, especially gang rape, so as to build internal ties.

For the victims and their families, rape does the opposite. The shame and degradation of rape rip apart social bonds. In societies where a family's honour rests on the sexual purity of its women, the blame for the loss of that honour often falls not upon the rapist, but the raped. In Bangladesh, where most of the victims were Muslim, the use of rape was not only humiliating for them as individuals but for their families and communities. The then prime minister, Mujibur Rahman, tried to counter this by calling them heroines who needed protection and reintegration. Some men agreed but most did not; they demanded sweeteners in the form of extra dowry payments from the authorities.

In Congo, despite the efforts of activists, rape still brings shame to the victim, says Ms. Margolis: "People can sit around and talk about the importance of removing the stigma in the abstract, but when it comes to their own wives or daughters or sisters, it is a different story." Many are rejected by their family and stigmatised by their community after being raped.

There is little prospect of justice for the victims of rape. Mr. Akayesu is one of the few people brought to book for rape in war. Though wartime rape is prohibited under the Geneva rules, sexual violence has often been prosecuted less fiercely than other war crimes. But the Balkan war-crimes court broke new ground by issuing verdicts treating rape as a crime against humanity. The convictions of three men for the rape, torture and sexual enslavement of women in the Bosnian town of Foca was a big landmark.

But in Congo the court system is in pieces. There have been fewer than 20 prosecutions of rape as either a war crime or a crime against humanity. The American Bar Association, which helps victims bring their cases to court in eastern Congo, has processed around 145 cases in the past two years. This has resulted in about 45 trials and 36 convictions based on domestic legislation, including a law introduced in 2006 to try and address the problem of sexual violence. Those who work with the survivors of rape in Congo have mixed feelings about the 2006 law. It has pricked consciences and made people more aware of their rights, concedes Ms. Margolis. It creates a theoretical accountability that could help punish perpetrators. But for women seeking justice, it has yet to have much impact. "There is still a glimmer of hope in people's eyes when they talk about the law. But the judicial and security systems need to be improved so that it can be applied better, or people may lose confidence in it," Ms. Margolis says.

Huge practical problems beset the legal system in Congo, says Richard Malengule, head of the Gender and Justice programme at HEAL Africa, a hospital in Goma. People have to walk 300km to get to a court. There is no money and no training for the police. Even if people are arrested, they are often released within a few days, in many cases by making a deal with the victim's family or the court. Those that go to jail often escape within days, Many prisons have no door—or corrupt guards.

Enduring effects

Given the parlous state of Congo's judiciary, raising the number of prosecutions may not help. Some want more international involvement. Justine Masika, who runs an organisation in Goma seeking justice for the victims of sex crimes, says Congolese courts must work with international ones in prosecuting rape. But "hybrid" courts require some commitment from the local government; Congo's rulers do not show much commitment to tackling rape. The International Criminal Court is investigating crimes, including rape, in Congo but gathering necessary evidence is hard.

Raising global awareness is another avenue; it helps lessen the stigma. Various UN resolutions over the past ten years have highlighted and condemned sexual violence against women and girls and called on countries to do more to combat it. But worthy language will not be enough.

Worse, the UN has faced criticism for failing to protect Congolese civilians from rape. In the Walikale attack, one UN official worries that the body is not meeting its obligations to protect civilians. He accepts that in remote places it is hard for peacekeepers to reach civilians, but insists that this does not justify the UN's failure in Walikale. He is dubious, too, about the investigations into the incident. "All these interviews, these investigations, what have they achieved? The survivors are interviewed again and again and again? Where does that get them?"

Without the presence of the UN, atrocities would be even more widespread, says Mr. Malengule. But in the long term, he says, more pressure must be put on Congo's government to tackle rape. At present, one aid worker laments, it just gets a lot of lip-service. The government would rather Congo were not known as the world's rape capital, but it shows little interest in real change.

Even when wars end, rape continues. Humanitarian agencies in Congo report high levels of rape in areas that are quite peaceful now. Again, it is hard to assess numbers. Figures for rape before the war do not exist. A greater willingness to report rape may account for the apparent increase. But years of fighting have resulted in a culture of rape and violence, says

Mr. Malengule. Efforts to reintegrate ex-combatants into society have been short and unsuccessful, with little follow-up to assess results. Add to that the dismal judicial system, and the outlook is grim.

It is bleaker still when you see how long rape's effects endure. Rebels seized Angelique's village in 1994. They slit her husband's throat. Then they bound her between two trees, arms and legs tied apart. Seven men raped her before she fainted. She does not know how many raped her after that. Then they shoved sticks in her vagina. Tissue between her vagina and rectum was ripped, and she developed a fistula. For 16 years she leaked urine and faeces. Now she is getting medical treatment, but justice is a distant dream.

Periodical and Internet Sources Bibliography

The following articles have been selected to supplement the diverse views presented in this chapter.

Julie Bindel	"A Weapon Against Half the World," *New Statesman*, March 8, 2010.
Stephanie Booth	"The Sex Crime No One Talks About," *Cosmopolitan*, March 2012.
Lucy Broadbent	"Rape in the US Military: America's Dirty Little Secret," *The Guardian* (Manchester, UK), December 9, 2011.
Jesse Ellison	"The Military's Secret Shame," *Newsweek*, April 11, 2011.
Erica Goode	"Researchers See Decline in Child Sex Abuse Rate," *New York Times*, June 29, 2012.
Kirk Johnson	"Newly Released Boy Scout Files Give Glimpse into 20 Years of Sexual Abuse," *New York Times*, October 19, 2012.
Amos Kamil	"Prep School Predators," *New York Times Magazine*, June 10, 2012.
Roni Caryn Rabin	"Men Struggle for Rape Awareness," *New York Times*, January 23, 2012.
Kelly Virella	"Chapter Two: Repeat Offenders: Many Claims of Abuse—Involving a Few Officers," *City Limits*, May/June 2011. www.citylimits.org.
Naomi Wolf	"A Culture of Coverup: Rape in the Ranks of the US Military," *The Guardian* (Manchester, UK), June 14, 2012.
Jim Yardley	"A Village Rape Shatters a Family, and India's Traditional Silence," *New York Times*, October 28, 2012.

CHAPTER 2

What Factors Contribute to Sexual Violence?

Chapter Preface

Embedded in the debates concerning the causes of, or contributing factors to, sexual violence are questions regarding why individuals behave in the ways they do. In particular, to what extent is behavior culturally determined or influenced and to what extent is it innate? While this debate surrounds all criminal activity to some extent, it is perhaps more frequently discussed in regard to sexual violence. In large part this may be related to the fact that sexual violence tends to target a more specific population than many other crimes. According to the Rape, Abuse & Incest National Network (RAINN), in 2003, nine out of every ten rape victims were women. Given these crimes' relatively narrow victim pool, it does not seem a big leap to wonder about the connection between cultural ideas of gender and the prevalence of such crimes.

Among feminist scholars and activists, there is little debate about whether cultural attitudes about women play at least some role in sexual violence. According to the Advocates for Human Rights, "Cultural norms that devalue women can combine with norms that value male dominance and aggressiveness to create a subculture that sanctions sexual violence." Comparing the evolution of a society's attitudes toward women and its rates of sexual violence offers some additional insight into this connection. As an example, in the United States, the number of rapes per capita declined by more than 85 percent from the 1970s to 2005, according to a 2006 *Washington Post* article. In this same time span, by nearly all measures—legally, politically, economically, socially—women's place in American society progressed considerably.

On the other hand, it is difficult to conclude that sexual violence is caused entirely by cultural factors, because if this were true, every member of a society with negative views of women would be a perpetrator of sexual violence. Thus, criminologists generally believe that individual factors are at least somewhat at play in sexual violence. According to the Center for Sex Offender Management, characteristics associated with sex offender recidivism (repeat offenses after serving time for a crime) include problems with intimacy, heightened hostility, emotional identification with children, and lifestyle instability. Sex offenders also frequently come from similar backgrounds, such as those with few resources, an unsupportive family environment, or an environment where physical violence was prevalent. Ultimately, though, as with most, if not all, human behaviors, both positive and negative, it is likely that sexual violence is the result of societal *and* individual factors. And thus, efforts to eliminate it must address them both. The authors of the viewpoints in this chapter explore the complexities of these contributing factors.

"*The characteristic way of thinking of [clergy] sex offenders has found its way into the collective psychic structure of an institution.*"

The Sexual Abuse of Children by Catholic Priests Is Rooted in Church Culture

Fran Ferder and John Heagle

In the following viewpoint, Fran Ferder, a Franciscan nun and clinical psychologist, and John Heagle, a priest and psychotherapist, argue that the seeming epidemic of sexual abuse in the Catholic Church, and the church's response to it, are indicative of a pathological institutional culture. They point to the church's policies on celibacy and ordination of women as illustrations of a collective psychology that prioritizes the obeying of its hierarchy above all else. Not only does this unhealthy mentality come through in the church's handling of the scandal, they say, but it may have contributed to the abuse itself.

As you read, consider the following questions:

1. What Vatican announcement do the authors seem to be responding to?

Fran Ferder and John Heagle, "The Inner Workings of a Hierarchy with a Sex Offender Mentality," *The National Catholic Reporter*, vol. 46, no. 21, August 6, 2010. Copyright © 2010 by the National Catholic Reporter. All rights reserved. Republished with permission.

2. According to Ferder and Heagle, how did clergy sex abusers react to accusations of abuse during psychological evaluations?

3. For which group of men do the authors say that "celibacy is easy"?

The Vatican announcement [in July 2010] that the attempted ordination of women is a "grave crime" to be dealt with according to the same procedures as the sexual abuse of minors exposes the way those running our church actually think. In attempting to explain revised norms to church canons, they reveal the legalistic inner workings of their minds, and affirm unsettling psychological patterns of thought.

Msgr. Charles Scicluna of the Vatican's Congregation for the Doctrine of the Faith, for example, speaking about the new codes July 15, [2010,] identified the sexual abuse of minors as an "egregious violation of moral law." His statement placed the emphasis on "violation of law." When all the words are parsed, and the nuances carefully articulated, it is law that has prominence.

What about the children? Should we not think of sexual abuse, in the first place, as an "egregious violation of children?"

Central Concern Made Apparent

This distinction is significant because it paints in bold letters the central concern of a hierarchical church whose first interest is ensuring its pronouncements are obeyed. A violated law and a violated child evoke, or ought to evoke, quite different emotional responses. Tears are generally not shed over a broken law. Perhaps this is why we have seen precious few tears among church leaders. They have been schooled to place obedience to the law above all else, with a tragic disconnect of empathy the predictable result.

Perhaps this is also why those who crafted the latest document can think of sexual abuse and the ordination of women in the same category of "grave crime." As long as both the abuse of minors and the ordination of women are avoided, the law is kept, and Rome is pleased.

A Familiar Mindset

We have conducted psychological evaluations of dozens of clergy sex abusers over the past 25 years [since the 1980s], becoming familiar with their style of cognitive processing. Similar to sex offenders in general, they typically deny responsibility, minimize the seriousness of their offenses, blame their victims, react with outrage when accused and redirect attention away from their behavior. They are self-centered and often exhibit a sense of grandiosity—a belief that they are above accountability. If this sounds familiar, it is because we have repeatedly—and sadly—been seeing it in the responses of church officials from the cathedrals of the United States to the basilicas of Rome.

A mentality is a way of thinking, a deeply ingrained pattern of perceiving, reasoning and decision-making. A sex-offender mentality is one that prompts defensive, self-serving, deceptive and blaming responses when faced with credible accusations of sexual crime. Unaware of their abnormal processing, sex offenders display a blindness that is central to the problem.

Chilling Similarities

Even more disconcerting, however, is that characteristics observed in the mentality of individual offenders can also be present in systems and institutions. The similarity in cognitive processing between actual offenders and the system that seeks to shield itself from their offenses is often chilling:

- "Holy Father, the people of God are with you and will not let themselves be influenced by the petty gossip of

The Church's Predictable Response

The Catholic Church is an authoritarian institution, modelled on the political structures of the Roman Empire and medieval Europe. . . . Its leaders are protected by a nimbus of mystery, pomp, holiness, and, in the case of the Pope, infallibility. . . . The hierarchy of such an institution naturally resists admitting to moral turpitude and sees squalid scandal as a mortal threat. Equally important, the government of the Church is entirely male.

It is not "anti-Catholic" to hypothesize that these things may have something to do with the Church's extraordinary difficulty in coming to terms with clerical sexual abuse.

Hendrik Hertzberg, New Yorker, *April 19, 2010.*

the moment" (Cardinal Angelo Sodano, former Vatican secretary of state, Easter 2010, St. Peter's Square).

- "Pupils told me on concert trips about what went on. But it didn't dawn on me from their stories that I should do something" (Fr. Georg Ratzinger, brother of Pope Benedict XVI, BBC, March 29 [2010]).

- Only 300 of about 3,000 sexual abuse cases spanning 50 years involved allegations of "genuine pedophilia" (Scicluna, the Congregation for the Doctrine of the Faith's promoter of justice, March 13 [2010]).

- "All we ask is that it be fair and that the Catholic church not be singled out for a horror that has cursed every culture, religion, organization, institution, school, agency and family in the world" (Archbishop Timothy Dolan of New York, March 28 [2010]).

- And the latest—the attempted ordination of women is a grave crime that ought to be treated with the same severity as the sexual abuse of a child.

Distorted Ways of Thinking

These and similar statements illustrate a mentality whereby the characteristic way of thinking of sex offenders has found its way into the collective psychic structure of an institution. The same "default" setting in the brain that triggers distorted mental processing prompts members of an entire group to think and respond in much the same way that sex offenders do. This "group think" inadvertently offers protection to actual sex offenders, and may have attracted them to the institution in the first place.

Let us be clear: We are not suggesting that church leaders are sex offenders. But we must name a tragic reality: Many of them think or respond the way sex offenders do when confronted with clergy sex abuse and its cover-up: They deny, defend and blame. They minimize and cover up. They become outraged when their abysmal handling of abuse cases is exposed. Most egregious of all, they display appalling deficits in empathy for victims: They turn to categorizing crimes when all people want is a heartfelt pastoral response from their leaders.

A Connection Worth Exploring

Celibacy is mandated for male church leaders. Women are excluded from sacramental leadership, thus creating an ecclesial environment that offers a perfect refuge for those whose sexual interests do not include women. Among them are the sexually disinterested, who simply don't pick up sexual cues in the environment. For these asexual men celibacy is easy—and so is failing to notice it when some of their brothers become sexual with minors. Since asexual individuals have a minimized capacity for intimate feelings, their affectivity is stunted, limiting their ability to experience the whole range of the most normal human feelings, including falling in love and feeling horrified over the abuse of a child. Women are a genuine threat to this world. They can expose it. Keeping them far away from the inner workings of the system is essential to its survival.

Rome has now connected the sexual abuse of minors and a ban on the ordination of women in one of its own documents. Perhaps those who crafted the document are on to something: The refusal to allow women into the inner sanctum of ecclesial power may well be related to clergy sexual abuse, and to the Vatican's impotence in addressing this crime in a truly pastoral way. Is the attempted ordination of women a crime, or is the real crime the refusal to allow it?

> "Sexual abuse is indeed horrible, but
> there is no empirical evidence that it is
> a uniquely, predominantly, or even
> strikingly Catholic problem."

What Went Wrong?

George Weigel

*In the following viewpoint, George Weigel, a Catholic theologian
and Distinguished Senior Fellow at the Ethics and Public Policy
Center in Washington, DC, responds to claims that the rampant
sex abuse in the Catholic clergy is rooted in church culture.
While conceding that the church did mishandle the abuse allegations and that some aspects of church culture may have contributed to the problem, ultimately, he contends, acts of sexual abuse
were violations by individuals of church teaching and their clerical vows. Weigel argues that instead of the church becoming less
strict, as many have suggested, it should actually be more so.*

As you read, consider the following questions:

1. In what context does most sexual abuse take place in
   the United States, according to the author?

2. Which Catholic Church members have particularly
   strengthened the handling of the abuse scandal, in
   Weigel's view?

George Weigel, "What Went Wrong?" *The Daily Beast*, April 2, 2010. Copyright © 2010
by The Daily Beast. All rights reserved. Republished with permission.

3. How many credible reports of sexual abuse of children in the US Catholic Church were there in 2009, according to the author?

Throughout what U.S. Catholics called the "Long Lent" of 2002, when every week seemed to bring revelations of clerical sexual abuse and its mishandling by the church's bishops, some observers suggested that this crisis was the by-product of some distinctive features of Catholic life: a celibate priesthood, a church governed by male bishops, a demanding sexual ethic. "Modernize" the church by changing all that, they argued, and these horrible problems would abate, even disappear.

Sexual abuse is indeed horrible, but there is no empirical evidence that it is a uniquely, predominantly, or even strikingly Catholic problem. The sexual abuse of the young is a global plague. In the United States, some 40 to 60 percent of such abuse takes place within families—often at the hands of live-in boyfriends or the second (or third, or fourth) husband of a child's mother; those cases have nothing to do with celibacy. The case of a married Wilmington, Delaware, pediatrician charged with 471 counts of sexual abuse in February has nothing to do with celibacy. Neither did the 290,000 cases of sexual abuse in American public schools between 1991 and 2000, estimated by Charol Shakeshaft of Virginia Commonwealth University. And given the significant level of abuse problems in Christian denominations with married clergy, it's hard to accept the notion that marriage is somehow a barrier against sexually abusive clergy. (Indeed, the idea of reducing marriage to an abuse-prevention program ought to be repulsive.) Sexual abusers throughout the world are overwhelmingly noncelibates.

Too many of the church's bishops failed to grasp the drastic measures required to address the sexual abuse of the young—that's obvious, and has been admitted by the bishops of the United States and two popes. Yet it is hard to see what these failures had to do with gender. Like others, many bishops had a misplaced faith in the power of psychiatrists and psychologists to "fix" sexual predators, thinking these men could be "cured" and quietly returned to ministry without damaging the church's reputation. In his recent scathing letter to the Catholic Church in Ireland, Pope Benedict XVI denounced bishops who were more concerned with protecting the church's image than with protecting vulnerable young people. It's a critique that was applicable decades ago in the United States—but the same criticism can be made of teachers-union leaders and state legislators today who ignore or try to bury reports of sexual abuse in America's public schools.

So, yes, aspects of clerical culture in the U.S. and elsewhere contributed to the problem, but that same deplorable circle-the-wagons instinct has warped the response to this plague in other sectors of society. The difference is that the Catholic Church in America has taken more rigorous action since 2002 to protect the young people in its care than any other similarly situated institution, to the point where the church is likely America's safest environment for young people.

There may be a grain of truth in the suggestion that women's perspectives on these issues would have helped mitigate the Catholic crisis of clerical sexual abuse and episcopal misgovernance: in the past the male clerical culture of Catholicism seems to have blunted in some Catholic clergy a natural and instinctive revulsion at the sexual abuse of the young—a revulsion, it is suggested, that a woman would immediately feel and act upon. But the sad, further truth is that there are no gender guarantees when it comes to sexual abuse: the physical and sexual abuse of young Irish girls in "Magdalene Asylums" decades ago was committed by religious sisters.

Nevertheless, it should also be noted that the U.S. church's handling of abuse and misgovernance since 2002 has been im-

Few Differences Found Between Priestly Abusers and Nonpriestly Abusers

Much remains to be learned about the causal factors or etiological determinants of sexual abuse of minors by priests and whether and how risk differs for priest versus non-priest offender populations. While widespread speculation has focused on issues such as homosexuality and the vow of celibacy, [author] John Loftus cautioned that "as regards the sexual misconduct of priests, we have plenty of theories, lots of anecdotal therapeutic explanations, but very little fact." Indeed, there has been relatively little focus on other potential etiological explanations, despite evidence that priests, as a group, appear similar to other males. [Researchers] found few differences between priest abusers and non-priest abusers when groups were matched on education and age. Indeed, [they] found loneliness, social isolation, and substance abuse to be common correlates of offending across priest and non-priest abusers. [Others] similarly contend that, while abusive priests tend to be older, better educated, and less antisocial than non-priest child molesters, they share common risk factors of sexual perpetration, including deviant sexual interests and alcohol abuse.

John Jay College of Criminal Justice Research Team,
The Causes and Context of Sexual Abuse of Minors by
Catholic Priests in the United States, 1950–2010, *May 2011.*

mensely strengthened by the insight and professional expertise of many women—just as we also ought to recognize that lay-women, single and married, are usually the teachers who make today's Catholic schools safe and successful. Moreover, women are the great majority of the volunteers and paid staff who make Catholic parishes both safe and vital. The notion that women don't have anything to do with how the Catholic Church operates confuses the Catholic Church with the higher altitudes of "the Vatican," and ignores how Catholic life is actually lived in America and Europe.

As for doctrine: what ought to be obvious about sexual abuse in the Catholic Church is that these grave sins and crimes were acts of infidelity, denials of the truths the church teaches. A priest who takes seriously the vows of his ordination is not a sexual abuser or predator. And if a bishop takes seriously his ordination oath to shepherd the Lord's flock, he will always put the safety of the Master's little ones ahead of concerns about public scandal. Catholic Lite is not the answer to what has essentially been a crisis of fidelity.

Since 2002, with strong support from then-cardinal Joseph Ratzinger (and from him still as Benedict XVI), the Catholic Church in America has developed and enforced policies and procedures to ensure the safety of the young that offer an important model for the world church. There were only six credible reports of sexual abuse of the young in the U.S. church last year. And while that is six too many in a church that ought to hold itself to the highest standards, it is nonetheless remarkable in a community of 68 million people.

What is essential throughout the world, however, is that the church become more Catholic, not less, John Paul II's "Theology of the Body" proposed an understanding of faithful and fruitful human love as an icon of God's inner life. That vision is far nobler, far more compelling, and far more humane than the sex-as-contact-sport teaching of the sexual revolution, the principal victims of which seem to be vulnerable young people. Those who are genuinely committed to the protection of the young might ponder whether Catholicism really needs to become Catholic Lite—or whether the Augean stables of present-day culture need a radical cleansing.

> *"Rape myths are not just a set of harmless beliefs, but are part of a larger destructive force that justifies violence in our culture."*

Misogynistic Social Norms Cause Sexual Violence

Janet Anderson

In this viewpoint, Janet Anderson, advocacy education director for the Washington Coalition for Sexual Assault Programs, argues that American culture encourages sexual violence through "rape myths" that blame the victim and excuse the perpetrator of such violence. Rape myths are muttered thoughtlessly by people in conversation, broadcast by the media, and misused in the criminal justice system. Contrary to the perception that these myths are harmless, she contends, they contribute to an environment that allows rape to continue; thus, eradicating these myths is critical to ending sexual violence.

As you read, consider the following questions:

1. According to Anderson, what was the original definition of "rape myths"?

Janet Anderson, "Rape Myths," *Research and Advocacy Digest*, vol. 9, no. 3, May 2007, pp. 1–3. Copyright © 2007 by the Washington Coalition of Sexual Assault Programs. All rights reserved. Republished with permission.

2. How do American cultural attitudes toward sexual violence contradict what most children are taught about being an adult, in the author's opinion?

3. How do rape myths influence the reporting of sexual violence, according to the author?

On any given day one can turn on a media story; read a newspaper; walk through the halls of justice; walk through a college or university campus; sit in a bar, playground, or just about anywhere else and most likely hear disparaging statements like, "Victims of rape lie or exaggerate," "she really wanted it, even if she said no," "how could he be assaulted," "she can't be raped, she's married to the guy," or any other similar sentiment. While most individuals in our society believe these to be true, and some might even say these are harmless beliefs or opinions, those of us working in the anti-rape field understand clearly that these are rape myths. And [we] know these myths all too well because [we] are out there fighting against them every single day.

Rape myths were first defined by [Martha] Burt in 1980 as "prejudicial, stereotyped or false beliefs about rape, rape victims, and rapists." Others further defined rape myths as "attitudes and beliefs that are generally false, yet widely held, and that serve to justify male sexual violence against women." However, a broader definition would include understanding that rape myths are central to the fundamental exercise of power and control, patriarchy, rape culture and ensuring the institutionalization of oppression of disenfranchised groups.

Excusing Perpetrators, Blaming Victims

We live in a culture that supports, excuses and encourages sexual violence and male sexual aggression. And what better way to preserve this system of power and control than to construct an entire mythology, or set of lies and stereotypes, that not only enables perpetrators to excuse or deny their sexual violence, but that also shifts the blame away from the perpetrator and places it squarely on the shoulders of the victim. When you think about it, this political and social arrangement that most people have bought into is actually quite brilliant. Growing up, we are taught that we can only be responsible for our own behavior, our own choices and our own actions. Yet, when it comes to sexual violence and rape myths, the victims are blamed and held responsible for the perpetrator's behaviors, choices and actions. This is completely counter-intuitive to everything we've been taught about being a capable adult, yet somehow it "makes sense" when it comes to rape.

When you hear people blaming victims, questioning their credibility, implying they deserved to be raped, say they enjoyed it, or when they trivialize someone's rape experience, do you ever wonder if they really understand what they are saying? Yet, because we live in a rape culture, it's nearly impossible not to have internalized these myths; indeed, we have been indoctrinated to believe them since the time we are born. They have become so integral to our way of thinking that most people don't understand the impact of what they are saying. For example, I recently overheard someone say that the woman central to the Duke Lacrosse case [a 2006 criminal investigation of three Duke University lacrosse players based on a false rape accusation] deserved to be raped even if the players weren't guilty because she was a stripper and a "ho." When I challenged that statement, the response I received was, "Well, that's my opinion and what I think is harmless. How can what I think hurt her?"

Beliefs Are Not Harmless

Rape myths are not just a set of harmless beliefs. Rape and rape myths are destructive forces. They do not fall on deaf ears, nor are they said in a vacuum. Although some people may think they are just "saying words" or holding on to innocuous beliefs, rape myths have profound impacts. They

A New Misogyny Has Surfaced in American Culture

One way in which things are much, much worse for women these days than 20 years ago is the sheer amount of virulent misogyny that is openly expressed, and tolerated, in our society.... [Conservative radio talk show host] Rush Limbaugh's comments about Sandra Fluke [a law student who testified before Congress in support of legally mandating insurance coverage of contraceptives] are only the most recent and notorious example of this new misogyny.... Female political leaders of both parties are held to a double standard and subjected to much humiliatingly sexist treatment. Many movies and TV shows, and reality shows especially, traffic in extremely sexist stereotypes ... Tabloids obsessively police the bodies of female celebrities and cruelly ridicule any famous woman who dares to go out in public looking less than perfect.

There's an extremely nasty edge to much of this running media commentary about women. It's not just garden variety sexism, because it's very conscious of itself and a lot of it is clearly driven by pure hatred.

Kathleen Geier,
Political Animal (blog), Washington Monthly,
March 11, 2012. www.washingtonmonthly.com.

hurt. They hurt individuals, they hurt survivors, they hurt families and they hurt communities. They encourage silence, shame and pain. They shift blame away from the perpertrator, and, ultimately, keep us believing that sexual violence is natural and normal. And, most assuredly, perpetrators count on us believing them in order to continue perpetrating sexual violence.

Much is at stake when most of our society supports and accepts these myths as truth: It allows perpetrators to deny and excuse their violence, it grants permission to not be held accountable, it allows for a system of social and economic control, it fosters opportunities to dehumanize whole groups of people, and it ultimately produces an environment where witnesses and bystanders get to remain neutral and disengaged.

Dismantling rape myths is critical to the work of ending rape. While we won't find many individuals who would stand up and claim that it is O.K. to rape, when people imply that victims deserve it, question a victim's credibility, or hold up rape myths and rape-supportive attitudes and beliefs as truth, that is exactly what they are saying.

Part of a Destructive Cultural Force

Because rape myths are so prevalent and institutionalized throughout all aspects of our society, we see them played out through pop culture, through the media, within our institutions and, unfortunately, within ourselves. They are evidenced every time a police officer approaches a victim with suspicion and doubt; when a prosecutor fails to take a case because he/she believes the victim isn't a "genuine victim" because the victim is a sex worker or a person with a developmental disability; and when family, friends and peers fail to support a survivor. They are evidenced when a survivor won't tell someone for fear of being judged, denigrated or told they deserved it; and they are evidenced by the tremendous amount of guilt, shame and isolation survivors feel.

So, it's up to us to set the record straight. It's up to us to listen to survivors and be there to support them. It's up to us to help them understand that the sexual assault had nothing to do with their clothing; it had nothing to do with how late they stayed out or how much they drank. And, hopefully, one day when they understand this they'll be able to let go of the guilt and shame they carry.

And it's up to us to continue educating our communities about the realities of rape myths—that rape myths are not just a set of harmless beliefs, but are part of a larger destructive force that justifies violence in our culture. And when they really get that rape myths are painful, when they get that these myths are being applied to a child, a mother, a father, a teenaged boy, a human being, hopefully then they will pause the next time they are about to say something disparaging about a rape survivor. That would truly be a good day.

> *"Exposure to non-violent or violent por-
> nography results in increases in both
> attitudes supporting sexual aggression
> and in actual aggression."*

Pornography Contributes to Sexual Violence

Gail Dines

*The following viewpoint is a statement given by Gail Dines dur-
ing a June 2010 congressional briefing on the harms of pornography. Dines, a professor of sociology and women's studies at
Wheelock College in Boston, explains that pornography has become deeply embedded in American culture, shaping the way
that men see both sex and women. Pornography's depiction of
women as sex objects whose sole purpose is for men's use and
abuse affects men's conception of women even when they are not
consuming pornography, Dines says, encouraging them to act out
what they see, thus increasing violence against women.*

As you read, consider the following questions:

1. According to Dines, how are those who criticize pornography often perceived in American culture?

Gail Dines, "Congressional Briefing on the Harms of Pornography," Gaildines.com, June
26, 2010. Copyright © 2010 by Gail Dines. All rights reserved. Republished with permission.

2. What does it mean to be a "real man" in pornography, as the author relates it?

3. In the study of scenes from fifty of the most frequently rented pornographic movies, what percentage does Dines say contained physical aggression?

Howard Stern regularly features pornography on his show, and for this he was the second highest paid celebrity in the world in 2007; Hugh Hefner's life with his blonde, young and embarrassingly naïve "girlfriends" is the topic of the hugely successful show, *The Girls Next Door* on E! Entertainment; retired mega-porn star Jenna Jameson has written a best-selling book; Miley Cyrus, the former Disney star who is a role model to young girls everywhere is photographed for *Elle* magazine, sprawled on a table wearing S/M [sadomasochism] gear; and students at Yale University invite pornographers to give talks on campus. I could go on, but these examples illustrate how porn has seeped into our everyday world and is fast becoming such a normal part of our lives that it barely warrants a mention.

A key sign that pornography is now deeply embedded in our culture is the way it has become synonymous with sex to such a point that to criticize pornography is to get slapped with the label "anti-sex". But sex in pornography is a carefully documented and orchestrated set of images, not a mere reflection of reality. Porn sex is a sex that is debased, dehumanized, formulaic and generic, a sex based not on individual fantasy, play or intimacy, but one that is the result of an industrial product created by men who get excited not by bodily contact but by profits.

Understanding that porn is an industry means that it needs to be seen as a business, whose product evolves with a specifically economic logic. This is a business with considerable political clout, with the capacity to lobby politicians, engage in expensive legal battles, and use public relations to influence public debate. Like the tobacco industry, this is not a simple matter of consumer choice; rather the business is increasingly able to deploy a sophisticated and well-resourced marketing machine, not just to push its wares but also to cast the industry's image in a positive light.

When I talk about pornography, I am often asked why I am getting so upset about pictures of naked women. Well, traditional *Playboy*-style images were bad enough in their sexism but anyone who is familiar with contemporary pornography knows that the days of naked women wearing coy smiles and not much else have long gone. Internet pornography today is filled with body-punishing sex where a woman is penetrated in every orifice by any number of men at the same time. As they pound away at her body, they call her vile, hateful names such as filthy whore, dirty slut, cumdumspter and worse, as a way to compound the degradation. Nothing is too painful or debasing for these women since, according to porn, they love it. . . .

The Commercial Documentation of Assault

It is important to stress that the issue is not artistic expression versus sexual repression. Porn is the commercial documentation of assault played out on real women's bodies who, like you and me, have real physical limits. Even the industry has said that shooting hardcore today is "difficult and demanding." The Adult Industry Medical Health Care Foundation, a non-profit organization that serves the sex industry, states that women in pornography are at risk for chlamydia and gonorrhea of the throat and/or eye/and or anus, hepatitis B, and vaginal and anal tears.

Pornography, like all media forms, tells stories about the world, but the stories it tells are of the most intimate in nature. It tells men that women exist solely for male use and abuse, that they like to be debased and are willing at any time and any place to submit to men's sexual demands. It tells men that they have a right of total and complete access to women's bodies, that they as men lack empathy and humanity and that they have no sexual integrity. To be a real man in pornography is to violate sexual boundaries and borders, and to see sex as making hate to a woman's body. Bled dry of intimacy, connection and emotion, porn sex is reduced to a technical, plasticized, formulaic generic act that men do to women as a way to demonstrate the power that they have over them.

Definite Effects

To argue, as the pornographers do, that pornography has no effect on its consumers is to ignore decades of research that explores how media images shape our cognition and behavior. To suggest that a man or boy can walk away from pornography unchanged is to ignore how we, as social beings, build our sexual identities, norms and values from the images and messages that pervade our culture. Media images help construct our mental map of the world and the way we make sense of our place in it. Today, pornography is the major form of sex education for boys, and as it seeps into mainstream media, for girls as well.

One area of controversy is the question of whether pornography causes rape. After reviewing the major studies in the area, Neil Malamuth, one of the most well-known psychologists studying the effects of porn, concluded that "experimental research shows that exposure to non-violent or violent pornography results in increases in both attitudes supporting sexual aggression and in actual aggression." In addition, in his own study Malamuth found that:

> When we considered men who were previously determined to be at high risk for sexual aggression . . . we found that those who are additionally very frequent users of pornography were much more likely to have engaged in sexual aggression than their counterparts who consume pornography less frequently.

America Has Been Pornified

In 2001, *Esquire* magazine described "the pornographication of the American girl" in its profile of a former pornographer. Four years later, author Pamela Paul testified before the U.S. Senate Judiciary Subcommittee on the Constitution about how our lives, relationships, and families have become "pornified," a term that became the title of her recently published book. More recently, the *Boston Globe* described the "pornification of America" this way:

"Not too long ago, pornography was a furtive profession—its products created and consumed in the shadows. . . . What is new and troubling, critics suggest, is that the porn aesthetic has become so pervasive that it now serves as a kind of sensory wallpaper, something that many people don't even notice anymore."

Some say that because of shifts in culture and technology, "pornography has already won."

Sadly, pornography "is so commonplace that for many it is merely an annoyance." It may indeed be "the new metaphor" and "the new universally shared experience." But pornography is not simply a matter of taste; it is a matter of harm that is magnified because today's pornography is more extreme and more readily available than ever.

Orrin G. Hatch,
Stanford Law & Policy Review, *June 5, 2012.*

Shaping How Men Approach Sex

Taken together, over forty years of research into pornography has demonstrated a link between pornography and sexual aggression against women. But it would be a mistake to see the effects of porn just in terms of rape, since studies show that many of the effects are subtle and cumulative. I have interviewed hundreds of men about their porn use and found that porn affects men in the following ways:

- It makes them want to emulate the sex they see in porn

- It makes them think that women in general enjoy porn sex

- It makes them feel like sexual losers because they can't perform like the men in porn

- It makes them angry at the women in their lives who refuse to perform porn sex

- It makes them less interested in real human beings and more interested in using porn

- It gets in the way of connection when they are having sex with their partners

- It cultivates a taste for harder and harder porn since they become desensitized and bored

Indeed, it is this last finding that is most alarming since it speaks to the need to keep increasing the level of cruelty against women as a way to keep consumers interested. As one porn producer told *Adult Video News*, the trade journal of the pornography industry, "People want more. . . . Make it more hard, make it more nasty, make it more relentless."

Violence Against All of Society

In one of the only studies on the content of contemporary pornography, it was found that the majority of scenes from 50 of the top-rented porn movies contained both physical and verbal abuse targeted against the female performers. Physical aggression, which included spanking, open-hand slapping and gagging, occurred in over 88% of scenes while expressions of verbal aggression, calling the woman names such as bitch or slut, were found in 48% of the scenes. The researchers concluded that "if we combine both physical and verbal aggression, our findings indicate that nearly 90% of scenes contained at least one aggressive act. . . ."

While pornography is, without question, a form of violence against women in its production and consumption, we also need to see it as a form of violence against boys. To expose boys to images of sexual cruelty is to rob them of their right to develop sexually in ways that are authentic and developmentally appropriate.

I want to say that as someone who has studied the pornography industry for over 20 years, I am still surprised that it has become so brutal this quickly. We are now in the midst of a massive social experiment, as no other generation has been so bombarded with pornographic images. We have had our sexuality and indeed our culture hijacked by a predatory industry that does not promote our sexual freedom but rather limits and constrains our imaginations and desires. As pornography increasingly becomes part of our sexual landscape, we limit our capacity for sexual intimacy and love. If we believe that, as a culture, we deserve more than what the pornographers offer, then we must begin to roll up our sleeves and get to work to wrestle back that which is rightfully ours.

| "Access [to pornography] is associated with substantial declines in rape victimization rates."

Pornography May Actually Deter Sexual Violence

Todd D. Kendall

Todd D. Kendall is a vice president at Compass LexEcon, a global economics consulting firm. In the following viewpoint, Kendall presents his own research that challenges the popular notion that consuming pornography increases sexual violence. In fact, he says, viewing pornography may actually substitute for sexual assault, thus, decreasing it. Among other evidence, he points to a decline in rapes correlating with a rise in Internet access, which made pornography more available to users than it had been, greatly increasing its consumption and, he argues, reducing actual sexual assaults.

As you read, consider the following questions:

1. What fraction of Internet users admitted to accessing an adult website within the month that a 2003 Nielsen Net Ratings survey was conducted, as reported by Kendall?

Todd D. Kendall, "Pornography, Rape, and the Internet," Clemson University, July 2007, pp. 3–7, 24–25. Reproduced by permission.

2. According to a 2006 source cited by the author, which age group is the largest consumer of Internet pornography?

3. By what percentage did rates of rape decline at the same time that there was a 10 percent increase in Internet access, according to Kendall?

The prefix *porno-* is derived from the Greek term for a prostitute; hence, it may be said that pornography is as old as the "world's oldest profession". Sexually explicit images were widespread in Classical Greek and Roman art. However, the social stigma placed on sexually explicit materials associated with the rise of Christianity in the first millennium A.D. led to prohibitively high increases in the non-pecuniary [nonmonetary] price of pornography for most individuals. Since then, improvements in communication and transportation technology over time have slowly lowered pecuniary prices, while changes in social mores have generally trended towards lower non-pecuniary prices.

However, these trends have generally been quite slow, and for most of the last two millennia, there has been no systematized recording of rape victimizations. These facts have stymied many attempts to use population-level data to estimate the effects of pornography consumption on rape.

By comparison, the arrival of the internet offered a rapid, quantum leap in pornography distribution. While bulletin board systems in the 1980s offered some distribution of erotic stories, the invention of the World Wide Web in 1993 and the first graphical browser, Mosaic, in 1995, allowed large numbers of technologically unsophisticated users to quickly download, view, and discreetly store pornographic photos and moving images on their home computers. Moreover, electronic distribution involves significantly lower marginal costs of production in comparison to paper or videotape copies, leading to a substantial increase in supply.

Increases in Internet Porn Use

Due to its decentralized nature, definitive statistics on internet content are necessarily error-prone. However, there is little doubt that the rise of the internet has led to significant increases in the consumption of pornography in the U.S. By October, 2003, Nielsen Net Ratings surveys indicated that one in four internet users admitted to accessing an adult web site within the month, spending an average of 74 minutes on such sites, and these figures do not include time spent on "amateur" porn sites nor downloads from peer-to-peer services, such as Kazaa, on which 73% of all movie searches in a recent survey were for pornographic films. Moreover, 12% of all internet websites, 25% of all search engine requests, and 35% of all peer-to-peer downloads are pornographic.

This technological innovation has not gone unnoticed by statutory authorities. Major provisions of the Communications Decency Act of 1996 attempted to strictly regulate internet pornography, although many of these provisions were later ruled unconstitutional. Currently, it is still unclear precisely how the "community standards" of decency upon which pre-internet obscenity laws were based will be interpreted and enforced in cyberspace, and there has been very little enforcement of obscenity regulations online.

While the fall in the pecuniary price of pornography due to the internet may have been constant across all groups of users, the fall in the non-pecuniary price has likely been highest among the young, who typically live with their parents. Before the arrival of the internet, these consumers' access to, and ability to discreetly store, sexually explicit materials was thus highly restricted. The privacy in consumption and storage allowed by electronic distribution increased the availability of pornography to younger age groups significantly. According to the internet traffic measuring service comScore, 70% of 18- to 24-year-old men visit adult sites each month. Statistics from 2006 find that the 12–17 age group is the largest demo-

More Porn Equals Less Rape

"Rates of rapes and sexual assault in the U.S. are at their lowest levels since the 1960s," says Christopher J. Ferguson, a professor of psychology and criminal justice at Texas A&M International University. The same goes for other countries: as access to pornography grew in once restrictive Japan, China and Denmark in the past 40 years, rape statistics plummeted. Within the U.S., the states with the least Internet access between 1980 and 2000—and therefore the least access to Internet pornography—experienced a 53 percent increase in rape incidence, whereas the states with the most access experienced a 27 percent drop in the number of reported rapes.

Melinda Wenner Moyer, Scientific American, *July 22, 2011.*

graphic consumer of internet pornography, and that 80% of 15–17 year olds admit to multiple exposures to hard-core pornography on the internet. By comparison, in most states, children under age 18 are prohibited from entering adult film houses or renting pornographic videos.

The Effects of Pornography on Rape

Crime in general has long stood as a challenge to economic analysis, given the view that many criminals are psychologically disturbed, and thus, potentially irresponsive to incentives. Rapists in particular are commonly believed to be "sick" or lunatics. However, a large body of psychological and sociological research has generally concluded that this view is false; therefore, there is a *prima facie* [clear] case that potential rapists may respond to price variation in complementary and substitute goods.

The production of pornography may be directly associated with sexual violence if the actors or other participants are involved without their consent, or are abused during production. However, the number of individuals producing pornography is much smaller than the number consuming it, so that if a significant effect exists, it seems more likely to arise from the "demand" than the "supply" side.

Since pornography is used to sexually arouse its consumer, this arousal may increase the demand for sex and/or for particular experiences associated with rape. Thus, pornography and rape may be economic complements. Moreover, repeated experiences with pornography can lead to conditioning, habituation, and desensitization that lower the inhibitions or psychic costs of rape to perpetrators. Pornography consumption may also have effects on cultural norms that lead to higher levels of rape, or lower women's self-esteem, a well-known risk factor for rape. For instance, the rise of internet pornography has been blamed for coarsening culture, and some feminist scholars have claimed that pornography enforces a male-dominated social hierarchy in which rape is more socially acceptable.

Pornography as a Substitute for Rape

On the other hand, consumption of pornography may reduce rape if they are economic substitutes. Consumers of pornography are often already aroused, and seek to use the material to relieve arousal. Thus, [one scholar] theorizes that if pornography is a complement for masturbation or consensual sex, then pornography consumption could also deter rapes. . . .

My analysis of the effects of the internet on rape victimization suggest[s] that internet access is associated with substantial declines in rape victimization rates, on the order of a 7.3% decline in rape from a 10 percentage point increase in internet access. Given the limited amount of data, and the potential for substantial measurement error, these results cannot be treated as fully definitive. However, if these results are spurious, and are actually driven by some omitted variable, that variable must be uncorrelated with crime generally, specific to young people, and concentrated in areas with relatively high male-to-female sex ratios. While there may be a few such variables, the most likely interpretation of the results seems to be that internet pornography is substituting for sexual violence.

A Decline in Rape

The results [of my research] suggest that potential rapists perceive pornography as a substitute for rape. With the mass market introduction of the World Wide Web in the late-1990s, both pecuniary and non-pecuniary prices for pornography fell. The associated decline in rape illustrated in the analysis here is consistent with a theory, such as that ... in which pornography is a complement for masturbation or consensual sex, which are themselves substitutes for rape, making pornography a net substitute for rape.

Given the limitations of the study, policy prescriptions based on these results must be made with extreme care. More research on other countries, other time periods, or using other methodologies or datasets is necessary before broad results can be stated with confidence. Nevertheless, the results of this simple study point to what may be important flaws in the previous literature, and suggest that liberalization of pornography access may not lead to increased sexual victimization of women.

> *"The encouragement of male aggression and the support of violence against women are regular features of popular rap music."*

Rap's Rape Culture: Ashley Judd Had a Point

James Braxton Peterson

James Braxton Peterson is the founder of Hip-Hop Scholars and an associate professor of English at Bucknell University in Pennsylvania. In the following viewpoint, he discusses the claim that rap and hip-hop music are misogynistic. While making a distinction between rap music and larger hip-hop culture and pointing out the positive intentions and effects of the latter, he concedes that popular rap music does often encourage violence against women. As a result of the commercialization of rap, he maintains, the genre reflects some of the more violent and sexist aspects of mainstream American culture.

As you read, consider the following questions:

1. For what reasons did Peterson choose to consider Ashley Judd's claim, rather than immediately dismiss it?

James Braxton Peterson, "Rap's Rape Culture: Ashley Judd Had a Point," *The Root*, April 12, 2011. Copyright © 2011 by the Washington Post Company. All rights reserved. Republished with permission.

2. What examples of hip-hop's positive cultural influences does the author cite?

3. Which artists does Peterson specifically name to illustrate his argument that rap music often reflects rape culture?

Actress Ashley Judd's new, highly publicized memoir, *All That Is Bitter & Sweet*, has been in stores for a week, and the actress is already making waves for some harsh judgments she made about rap music in the book. Judd wrote that she was upset when she saw that Snoop and Diddy were performing at the MTV World AIDS Day concert because "most rap and hip-hop music—with its rape culture . . . is the contemporary soundtrack of misogyny."

While many of us who follow, love and consider ourselves cultural constituents of hip-hop might concede that some rap music is undeniably misogynistic, we also stand up for it when we feel it's being unfairly attacked. I have regularly defended hip-hop culture from its detractors, and upon hearing Judd's sweeping condemnation—from which she later backed down after harsh criticism from The Roots drummer ?uestlove and others—I was ready to assume my normal position.

But she is not your usual hip-hop-hating suspect (think Bill O'Reilly). She's a noted progressive, and her work around the world speaks for itself, so instead of a knee-jerk response, I considered the possibility that her claim was true—not of hip-hop culture, but of rap music.

There's a regularly stated but not always understood distinction between rap music and hip-hop culture. Rap music is one element of hip-hop culture, which is a broader, generational phenomenon that includes a number of artistic elements, ways of being and speaking, and various social elements such as fashion and a particularly entrepreneurial spirit.

While rap music derives from the continuum of black oral and folk traditions, it, like other black musical forms, has been

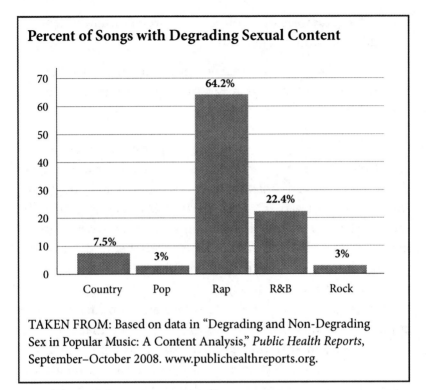

Percent of Songs with Degrading Sexual Content

Country 7.5% | Pop 3% | Rap 64.2% | R&B 22.4% | Rock 3%

TAKEN FROM: Based on data in "Degrading and Non-Degrading Sex in Popular Music: A Content Analysis," *Public Health Reports*, September–October 2008. www.publichealthreports.org.

co-opted and commodified by mainstream America. In some of its most commercial forms, rap music is misogynistic, consumeristic and violent. And yes, it also reflects the rape culture that is a part of popular American culture.

Hip-hop culture, on the other hand, actually counters the rape culture of rap music in some interesting and powerful ways. Consider the work of Salamishah Tillet, founder of A Long Walk Home, or see Byron Hurt's *Beyond Beats and Rhymes* or Immortal Technique's "Dance With the Devil" for ready references. And we should laud artists like Snoop or Diddy for their attempts to support vital efforts such as the YouthAIDS movement, because although they may be (or have been) guilty of contributing to America's rape culture, their potential to shine light on these very issues is reflected in their influence on popular culture in general.

Three years ago on *Larry King Live*, Snoop said, "In the past I've always made music that was very insulting to women, because that's what I was taught. That's what I was brainwashed not to know. As I get older, and with my wife and my daughter and my mother and my grandmother, I tend to make more records that are . . . aimed at telling the woman how beautiful she is and how she's appreciated and how I apologized for being so brainwashed and not knowing that I'm supposed to respect a woman."

Snoop's interview on *Larry King Live* should give us all hope that we can address misogyny in American society. The term "rape culture" seems strong, but the challenges with which we are confronted are both formidable and frightening. The facts: 17.6 percent of women in the United States have survived a completed or attempted rape. Of these, 21.6 percent were younger than age 12 when they were first raped, and 32.4 percent were between the ages of 12 and 17.

Of course, these are figures based only on those women who were brave enough to report. The vast majority of rapes and sexual assaults go unreported. And the vast majority of perpetrators are never brought to justice. In *Transforming a Rape Culture*, Emilie Buchwald, Pamela Fletcher and Martha Roth define rape culture as "a complex of beliefs that encourages male aggression and supports violence against women."

Tragically, rape is common in American culture, and rap music sometimes reflects the rape culture of American society. The encouragement of male aggression and the support of violence against women are regular features of popular rap music. Check out this verse from Notorious B.I.G. in "Dead Wrong": "Biggie Smalls for mayor, the rap slayer/The hooker layer . . . Hail Mary full of grace/Smack the b--ch in the face/ Take her Gucci bag and the North Face/Off her back, jab her if she act funny with the money/Oh you got me mistaken, honey/I don't wanna rape ya/I just want the paper." Jay-Z's verse on Kanye West's "Monster" alludes to raping and pillaging.

Although these lyrics should be ascribed to the artistic personas of these major hip-hop figures, I still reserve the right to critique, challenge and hold the authors of these artistic personas accountable for their music, especially if it is contributing to one of our greatest social challenges: gender equality and the freedom of women *not* to live in fear of violent assault.

That said, rapping specifically about rape is not what rape culture is all about. The ways in which some rappers promote attitudes that normalize sexual violence against women and children are the more common culprits of rap's rape culture. Consider these lines from West's verse in "Monster": "I put the p--sy in a sarcophagus/Now she claiming I bruise her esophagus." I am more than willing to grant artistic license to any of these rappers, as long as they are willing to be publicly accountable for the ways in which these verses promote attitudes and mentalities that contribute to rap's rape culture—as Snoop did on *Larry King Live.*

When Jay-Z signed Jay Electronica to Roc Nation label, it seemed like a triumph of underground hip-hop culture—the talented Jay Electronica, along with Jay-Z's formidable business and promotional acumen, could change the game for the better. Instead, the rapper has elected to use some troubling language in his live performances, polling his audiences to inquire if women "like being choked during sexual intercourse." Many feminist bloggers and activists challenged Jay Electronica directly.

For the survivors of violent sexual assault and for those of us who understand that sexual assault against women is a critical problem for all of us, this sort of thing is simply unacceptable. Maybe I am sensitized to this because my daughter just turned 10. But I'm also aware that even though individuals must be responsible for their own acts, too many are susceptible to subtle (and unsubtle) cues—from pop culture and the public sphere—that subject women to male dominance, and reaffirm the sexism and misogyny that lead to sexual violence against women.

That we, myself included, are always ready to defend hip-hop is a good thing—I think. Hip-hop cannot be the scapegoat for every talking head who is looking for an easy way to dismiss and degrade youth culture or black music. But rap and the industry that has developed through its popularity must be held accountable for its contributions to the world—and that includes any role that the industry might play in the construction and cultivation of rape culture in society. If you don't want to hear it from Ashley Judd, then maybe you can hear it from me.

Periodical and Internet Sources Bibliography

The following articles have been selected to supplement the diverse views presented in this chapter.

James Carroll — "Mandatory Celibacy at the Heart of What's Wrong," *National Catholic Reporter*, June 11, 2010.

Raquel Cepeda — "Stop Encouraging Sexual Assault of Our Young Black and Latina Girls," *CNN Wire* (blog), February 15, 2012. http://news.blogs .cnn.com.

Nancy Gibbs — "Sex, Lies, Arrogance: What Makes Powerful Men Behave So Badly?," *Time*, May 30, 2011.

Sean Gregory — "Penn State of Mind," *Time*, December 12, 2011.

Hendrik Hertzberg — "Indulgence," *New Yorker*, April 19, 2010.

Amanda Hess — "Is Sexual Violence on TV OK If the Heroine Is Tough?," *Slate*, August 31, 2012. www.slate .com.

Christopher Kaczor — "Celibacy Isn't the Problem," Catholic Answers, September 2010. www.catholic.com.

Sigrid Rausing — "The Vicious Cycle of Porn and Abuse," *New Statesman*, November 15, 2010.

Jason Schreier — "Playing the Rape Card: 'Media Psychiatrist' Ratchets Up Anti-videogame Rhetoric," *Wired*, February 11, 2011. www.wired.com.

Lisa Shannon — "No, Sexual Violence Is Not 'Cultural,'" *New York Times*, June 25, 2010.

Women's Health Journal — "Rape Simulator Games and the Normalization of Sexual Violence," January–June 2010.

OPPOSING
VIEWPOINTS®
SERIES

CHAPTER 3

How Does Society Respond to Sexual Violence?

Chapter Preface

Strategies for the prevention of crime often involve punishing those who commit it, and sexual violence is no exception. On an individual level, punishing the perpetrator of sexual violence is intended to bring some sense of justice to the victim. On a societal level, it is meant to act as a deterrent, thus preventing future crime. But penalties for committing acts of sexual violence vary widely—in part, because of the spectrum of such crime.

In the United States, the United Kingdom, and Canada, the maximum sentence for rape is life imprisonment. Sentences for rape in Sweden depend on the severity. "Minor rape," in which no violence or threat is used but the victim is incapacitated in some way, results in a maximum four-year prison sentence whereas for the most severe form, "gross rape," the maximum penalty is ten years of imprisonment. "Ordinary rape," the middle category, in which some violence may have been used, carries a maximum penalty of six years in prison.

Outside of Western society, legal responses to rape reflect very different cultural attitudes toward the crime itself and the parties involved. A report on the Arabic news network Al Jazeera explains, "In some societies, including several in the Arab world, the loss of a woman's virginity outside of marriage is considered a dishonour to her family." Thus, in many such societies, the rape victim herself is punished for the rape. The Women's Islamic Initiative in Spirituality and Equality says that in many Muslim societies, "women will face discrimination instead of the recognition and vital assistance they need after being abused. Some rape victims are murdered by relatives because the violation of a woman's chastity is viewed as an attack to their family's honor." As a means of restoring a woman's honor, some countries, such as Jordan and Morocco, allow a convicted rapist to avoid prosecution if he agrees to marry his victim.

Clearly, there is a broad diversity of legal responses to sexual violence across the globe, reflecting an equally broad spectrum of cultural ideas, attitudes, and values. Still, there seems to be some agreement that sexual violence must be sanctioned in order to reduce and eventually eradicate such crimes. The viewpoints in this chapter address society's responses to sexual violence.

| *"The Holy Father needs to directly an-*
| *swer questions, in a credible forum,*
| *about his role . . . in the mismanage-*
| *ment of the clergy sex abuse crisis."*

The Pope Participated in the Cover-up of Sex Abuse by Catholic Priests

The National Catholic Reporter

In the following viewpoint, the editors of the National Catholic Reporter *(NCR) call on Pope Benedict XVI (who resigned in February 2013) to honestly explain his role in the Catholic Church's cover-up of sex abuse by priests. The NCR editors point to Vatican statements that have gradually admitted more responsibility, after original claims that transfers of abusive priests from parish to parish were isolated incidents. Even now, the authors say, the pope is not being completely forthright, despite solid evidence that he oversaw such transfers when he was the archbishop of Munich, Germany. Although the church leadership is beginning to take responsibility for the crisis, the authors note, its apologies are too little, too late.*

"Credibility Gap: Pope Needs to Answer Questions," *National Catholic Reporter*, March 26, 2010. Copyright © 2010 by National Catholic Register. All rights reserved. Republished with permission.

As you read, consider the following questions:

1. What has been the extent of Pope Benedict's personal response to the sex abuse crisis, according to the authors?

2. In what year did the *National Catholic Reporter* first report on clergy sex abuse?

3. Which document did US bishops unveil in 2002 after meeting in Dallas?

The Holy Father [Pope Benedict XVI] needs to directly answer questions, in a credible forum, about his role—as archbishop of Munich (1977–82), as prefect of the Congregation for the Doctrine of the Faith (1982–2005), and as pope (2005–[2013])—in the mismanagement of the clergy sex abuse crisis.

We urge this not primarily as journalists seeking a story, but as Catholics who appreciate that extraordinary circumstances require an extraordinary response. Nothing less than a full, personal and public accounting will begin to address the crisis that is engulfing the worldwide church. It is that serious.

To date [March 2010], as revelations about administrative actions resulting in the shifting of clergy abusers from parish to parish emerge throughout Europe, Pope Benedict XVI's personal response has been limited to a letter to the Irish church. Such epistles are customary and necessary, but insufficient.

With the further revelations March 26 [2010] by *The New York Times* that memos and meeting minutes exist showing that Benedict had to be at least minimally informed that an abuser priest was coming into the archdiocese of Munich and that he further had been assigned without restrictions to pastoral duties, it becomes even more difficult to reconcile the strong language of the pope in his letter to Irish bishops and his own conduct while head of a major see.

Suspending Disbelief

No longer can the Vatican simply issue papal messages—subject to nearly infinite interpretations and highly nuanced constructions—that are passively "received" by the faithful. No longer can secondary Vatican officials, those who serve the pope, issue statements and expect them to be accepted at face value.

We were originally told by Vatican officials, for example, that in the matter of Fr. Peter Hullermann, Munich Archbishop Joseph Ratzinger [who later became Pope Benedict XVI] approved the priest's transfer to the archdiocese, but had no role in the priest's return to parish ministry, where he again molested children. Rather, it was Fr. Gerhard Gruber, archdiocesan vicar general at the time, who, according to a March 12 [2010] Vatican statement, has taken "full responsibility" for restoring the priest to ministry. Gruber, subsequent to his statement, has not made himself available for questions.

We are told, moreover, that the case of Hullermann is the single instance during Ratzinger's tenure in Munich where a sexually errant priest was relocated to a parish where he could molest again. If true, this would be a great exception to what, in the two-and-a-half decades *NCR* has covered clergy abuse in the church, has been an ironclad rule: Where there is one instance of hierarchical administrative malfeasance, there are more.

Given memos and minutes placing the pope amid the discussions of the matter, we are asked to suspend disbelief even further.

Context of Mismanagement

The first reported clergy sex abuse stories, dating back in *NCR* to 1985, focused on the misconduct of priests who had been taken to court by parents of molested children—parents who had gone to church officials, but received no solace. Instead, what they received from church officials was denial and counter accusation.

A Dishonest Apology

[Pope] Benedict's apology [in his March 2010 letter to the Catholics of Ireland] gives the impression that he heard about abuse only recently, and it presents him as a fellow victim. . . . But Benedict's infamous 2001 letter to bishops around the world ordered them to keep sexual abuse allegations secret under threat of excommunication—updating a noxious church policy, expressed in a 1962 document, that both priests accused of sex crimes and their victims "observe the strictest secret" and be "restrained by a perpetual silence."

Sinead O'Connor, Washington Post, *March 28, 2010.*

Almost from the beginning of the coverage of these trials, it was clear the clergy sex abuse story had two consistent components: the abusing priest and the cover-up by the bishop.

The story grew as more survivors of abuse came forward. What soon became evident was that this was not primarily a story of wayward priests, but of an uncannily consistent pattern by individual bishops. In nearly every instance, bishops, faced with accusations of child abuse, denied them, even as they shuffled priests to new parishes, even as they covered up their own actions.

Public Outrage

The story was first flushed out in the United States and soon across Canada. By the year 2000, sex abuse accusations were turning up across the globe. In the United States, the scandal flared anew in 2002 when a judge released thousands of pages of documents dealing with the sex abuse scandal in the Boston archdiocese. Suddenly, ordinary Catholics had access to the patterns involved in the cover-up and to the unfiltered language of memos and legal depositions and letters that outlined how church officials sought to protect perpetrators and marginalize their victims. All at once, the public outrage was commensurate with the hierarchy's outrageous behavior. The story would repeat itself around the country: Wherever documents were released or legal authorities conducted investigations, the depth of clerical depravity and the extent of hierarchical cover-up were far greater than previously acknowledged by church authorities.

Knowing they had an unprecedented crisis of credibility and facing potential multibillion-dollar liability, the U.S. bishops met in Dallas in June 2002. The whole world, represented by more than 800 members of the press, was watching.

There the prelates unveiled what came to be a "Charter for the Protection of Children and Young People." It was intended to protect children from molestation, establishing a "one strike and you're out" policy for offending priests. It did nothing, however, to hold accountable individual bishops who engineered the cover-up.

By early 2001, responsibility for managing the church's response to the ongoing crisis was delegated to the Congregation for the Doctrine of the Faith, headed by Cardinal Ratzinger. The Vatican, by then, viewed the crisis as beyond the boundaries of any one national church.

The Crisis Crosses Borders

In the last decade the story has not gone away. Rather it has continuously reared its head in nation after nation, especially in those countries with a free press and independent judicial system. A dominant characteristic of this story is that where and when it has emerged it has done so without the aid of church hierarchy. To the contrary, it has taken lawsuit after lawsuit, investigative report after investigative report, to bring this horrendous story to necessary light.

Another part of the pattern of this dispiriting tale is that church officials have never been in front of the story. Always late, always responding, and, therefore, at every step of the way losing credibility. This seemed to be the case once again with Benedict's pastoral letter to Irish Catholics.

By the time he issued the letter, the story had moved to his native country, Germany, and had touched him personally. In the past two months [February–March 2010], there have been more than 250 accusations of sex abuse in Germany. From the German Catholic viewpoint, the pope's failure to mention anything about these abuse cases has pained them deeply and added to suspicions that the former archbishop of Munich has lost touch with his people.

Inexorably, a story that began with reports on trials in a few U.S. cities a quarter century [around 1985] back has now moved up the Catholic institutional ladder—from priests to bishops to national bishops' conferences and to the Vatican itself. This last step is the one we see emerging this month. The new focus is unlikely to end anytime soon.

Time for Answers

The focus now is on Benedict. What did he know? When did he know it? How did he act once he knew?

The questions arise not only about his conduct in Munich, but also as prefect of the Congregation for the Doctrine of the Faith. A March 25 [2010] *Times* story, citing information from bishops in the United States, reported that the Vatican had failed to take action against a priest accused of molesting as many as 200 deaf children while working at a school from 1950 to 1974. Correspondence reportedly obtained by the paper showed requests for the defrocking of the priest, Fr. Lawrence Murphy, going directly from U.S. bishops to Ratzinger, then head of the Congregation for the Doctrine of Faith, and Cardinal Tarcisio Bertone, now the Vatican secretary of state. No action was taken against Murphy.

A Distressing Logic

Like it or not, this new focus on the pope and his actions as an archbishop and Vatican official fits the distressing logic of this scandal. For those who have followed this tragedy over the years, the whole episode seems familiar: accusation, revelation, denial and obfuscation, with no bishop held accountable for actions taken on their watch. Yes, there is a depressing madness to this story. Time after time, this is a story of institutional failure of the deepest kind, a failure to defend the Gospel of Jesus Christ, a failure to put compassion ahead of institutional decisions aimed at short-term benefits and avoiding public scandal.

The strategies employed so far—taking the legal path, obscuring the truth, and doing everything possible to protect perpetrators as well as the church's reputation and treasury—have failed miserably.

We now face the largest institutional crisis in centuries, possibly in church history. How this crisis is handled by Benedict, what he says and does, how he responds and what remedies he seeks, will likely determine the future health of our church for decades, if not centuries, to come.

It is time, past time really, for direct answers to difficult questions. It is time to tell the truth.

"Benedict refused to ignore the [sex abuse] issue [and] was heartfelt in his sorrow and his disappointment."

Grace Under Fire

Brian Bethune

In the following viewpoint, Brian Bethune, a senior writer for the Canadian weekly newsmagazine Maclean's, *defends Pope Benedict XVI against criticisms of his handling of the Catholic sex abuse scandal, both as the pope and before that as archbishop of Munich, Germany. Bethune points out that most of the sex abuse cases coming to light took place before Benedict held the office of Pope John Paul II's chief disciplinarian. Compared with John Paul II, Bethune says, Benedict XVI has done much more to crack down on abusive clergy and been more forthright in informing the public about the scandal and apologizing to abuse victims. Pope Benedict XVI resigned on February 28, 2013. Jorge Mario Bergoglio, the cardinal archbishop of Buenos Aires, Argentina, was elected on March 13, 2013, as his successor, Pope Francis I.*

As you read, consider the following questions:

1. When was Peter Hullermann convicted of sexually abusing children in Germany, according to Bethune?

Brian Bethune, "Grace Under Fire," *Maclean's*, December 9, 2010. Copyright © 2010 by Maclean's Magazine. All rights reserved. Republished with permission.

2. Which country does the author say was "never the most Catholic-friendly country at the best of times"?

3. Which abusive priest was ignored by Pope John Paul II but removed by Pope Benedict XVI early in his papacy, according to Bethune?

There is always, in the spiritual and political life of the Roman Catholic Church, a fire smouldering somewhere: minority Christians under persecution here, an abortion initiative in a Catholic country there, rebellious laity, scandalous clergy. So Pope Benedict XVI had no particular reason, on New Year's Day [2010], to foresee that the long-running clerical child sexual abuse scandal would suddenly burn white-hot, and spread far outside the confines of his Church. But as the penitential season of Lent began in February, hundreds more victims surfaced with their harrowing stories, not only in Ireland and the U.S., the epicentres of the scandal, but across Europe, including Benedict's native Germany.

This time it was more than the original crimes that angered the faithful and outsiders alike. The focus was increasingly on the cover-up—the swearing of victims to secrecy, the shuffling of pedophile priests to fresh starts (and fresh opportunities) in unsuspecting parishes—and the way that cover-up touched the papacy itself. Questions were raised in the media and among Catholics about Benedict's role, before he became pope, in determining the Vatican's treatment of predatory clergy, a response widely condemned as ineffectual at best and criminally negligent at worst. Benedict found himself launched on an *annus horribilis* [a horrible year] that would prove as awful as any experienced by a pope in modern times.

In March [2010], the Pope became caught up in the German part of the scandal. As Cardinal Joseph Ratzinger, archbishop of Munich in 1980, he had reportedly approved the transfer of confessed pedophile priest Peter Hullermann to

Abuse Cases Dropped Under Ratzinger

It has been alleged that Pope Benedict XVI has been at the forefront of a cover-up of sexual abuse cases within the Catholic Church since he (the then Cardinal Ratzinger) served as the Prefect of the Congregation for the Doctrine of the Faith (CDF), his post before becoming Pope.... [But] reports of sexual abuse peaked in 1981, the year Pope John Paul II appointed Cardinal Ratzinger to the CDF. Since then the number of abuse cases alleged per 1,000 priests has dropped from 9 to 1.

Matt Glassman,
Examiner.com, April 9, 2010.

therapy. After being treated for only a few days, Hullermann returned to pastoral duties and abused more children. He was finally convicted of sexual abuse in 1986. Benedict's defenders, who dismissed the Hullermann allegations as an attempt to smear the Pope's reputation, were left reeling when it emerged in mid-March that Hullermann, now out of jail, was still practising as a priest. (He was immediately suspended from his duties.)

Ratzinger's failure to defrock Lawrence Murphy, one of the most notorious pedophiles in the U.S. Church, who had molested 200 deaf boys in Wisconsin during the 1960s and '70s, also drew fire. Ratzinger halted a Church trial in 1996 after Murphy wrote to him to beg for mercy because of his poor health. The cardinal, noting no criminal charges had been laid, acceded. Murphy was allowed to die a priest, and was buried in his vestments.

By summer the Pope was facing calls for his resignation, massive and hostile media attention, and the prospect of a harrowing September visit to Britain. Never the most Catholic-friendly country at the best of times, the homeland of author Christopher Hitchens and Geoffrey Robertson, the human rights jurist whose new book sets out the case for prosecuting Benedict for obstruction of justice, promised to be a papal nightmare of bad press, sullen Catholics and angry demonstrators. Michael Higgins, one of the most prominent lay Catholic intellectuals in Canada, was there for the visit. Among the organizers and senior churchmen involved, he says, "determinedly happy faces hid almost universal worry."

But a funny thing happened on the way to Benedict's Waterloo.[1] Catholic rage, if not outsiders' condemnation, started to abate, as the faithful recalled that Benedict had done far more than his predecessor, the charismatic John Paul II, to crack down on abusive clergy and, just as important, was much more open about the scale of the problem, even if not to the extent some would wish. And they realized, too, that the cover-up cases now being revealed were, on the whole, old cases, indicating that steps taken by the Church in the 1980s and after—including by Ratzinger, the Vatican's chief disciplinarian under John Paul—had borne fruit.

Benedict, after all, was the Pope who had decried the "filth" that was encrusting his Church and who met with victims time and again. "I think the British tour went well," Higgins remarks, "because Benedict refused to ignore the issue. He was heartfelt in his sorrow and his disappointment. I think he gets the message—realizes how huge this issue is and how much damage was done—far more than John Paul did." Early in his papacy, Benedict removed from active ministry the Mexican sexual abuser Marcial Maciel Degollado, who had simply been ignored during the papacy of his good friend John Paul. Higgins calls it "the most egregious example of tolerated corruption in John Paul's time, and Benedict ended it."

---

1. Waterloo was the Belgian city where Napoléon Bonaparte was finally defeated in 1815. It has since come to connote someone's final downfall.

The Pope too seems to have felt that the storm, at least as it swirled about him personally, was abating in the autumn. Or perhaps, at 83, he's in a hurry to accomplish his oft-indicated aim of reconciling faith and reason and gaining a greater presence for the Church in the public square. Instead of ducking the headlines, Benedict collaborated on a wide-ranging book with a sympathetic German author, Peter Seewald, in which the Pope asserted, among other matters, that resignation on health grounds was a viable option for popes and—far more controversially—that the need to prevent diseases like AIDS could outweigh the Church's blanket opposition to condoms.

He gave the startling (for a pope) example of a male prostitute wearing one for a client's sake. A Vatican spokesman later confirmed that for Benedict, the use of condoms by people infected with HIV, female or male, could be "the first step of responsibility, of taking into consideration the risk to the life of the person with whom there are relations." Though Benedict emphatically did not alter official Church teaching—still opposed to contraceptive use—his words angered some conservative Catholics. They were welcomed by many others, including clerics and health care workers in Africa, where the AIDS problem is worst—and where Catholicism is booming.

The Christian liturgical year began anew on Nov. 28 [2010] with the First Sunday of Advent. Pope Benedict XVI could have left his old, horrible year, on the quiet. But that doesn't seem to be his style.

*"The cover-up of child abuse may be
rife in our society."*

Cover-ups of Child
Sexual Abuse Are Rife
in American Society

Nick Bryant

Nick Bryant is the author of Franklin Scandal: A Story of Powerbrokers, Child Abuse, and Betrayal. *In the following viewpoint, he discusses revelations of rampant sexual abuse and
cover-ups at respected institutions, noting his own lack of shock
compared to the reactions of most Americans. Bryant recounts
some of his research on the abuse cases and elaborate cover-ups
that followed them, and the resistance he met upon attempting
to publish his findings. Still, he says, Americans need to wake up
to the fact that there is sexual abuse in every corner of society,
and it must be brought to light.*

As you read, consider the following questions:

1. Which report provoked the author's interest in the issue
   of child trafficking?

Nick Bryant, "Child Sexual Abuse's Second Shame," *USA Today Magazine*, January 2012.
Copyright © 2012 by USA Today Magazine. All rights reserved. Republished with permission.

2. Of the more than five hundred sexual abuse lawsuits against Catholic dioceses that Judge Schiltz worked on, how many does he estimate were based on false accusations, as reported by Bryant?

3. According to Bryant, what is suggested by Penn State's refusal to release the records from its 1998 inquiry into coach Jerry Sandusky?

The [2011 sex abuse] scandals at Penn State and Syracuse universities, Brooklyn's Poly Prep Country Day School, Fenway Park, and now the Amateur Athletic Union, along with the intimations of possible cover-ups of child sexual abuse, have citizens shocked and outraged. However, these recent allegations only are the latest variations on a theme of abuse by churches and respected organizations like the Boy Scouts.

Pedophilia seems to exist in a distant parallel universe that is antithetical to the universe of Little League, Disneyland, and the other hallmarks of wholesome, youthful Americana, but the current allegations of pedophilia and the possibility of its cover-up just may be waking up Americans to the reality that this universe may not be as distant as they once thought.

I have shared the outrage at the reports of sexual abuse but, unlike most people, I have not been shocked, because of my research over the last decade. Prior to 2002, I had written extensively on children's issues, and then I stumbled across a 1987 U.S. Customs report on a "child abuse investigation" that the agency was conducting, and it described child abuse of the most horrific nature.

Two men connected to the investigation had been arrested and charged with multiple counts of child abuse, and six children, whose ages ranged from two to six years old, had been placed in Florida's child protective services. The investigation ultimately was quashed by Federal authorities (who should not have had jurisdiction in this situation), and the two men were released from jail and the charges dropped. I was stunned by the report, and it triggered my prolonged odyssey into the depths of child trafficking in America.

Cover-ups Are Rife

Although witch-hunt hysteria is to be avoided when these accusations come to light, it is important to consider that the cover-up of child abuse may be rife in our society. Sexual-abuse victims often are very reluctant to come forward because they frequently are branded as liars, opportunists, and gold diggers. Such denunciations already have been leveled against the alleged victims of Penn State's [assistant football coach] Jerry Sandusky and Syracuse University's [assistant basketball coach] Bernie Fine.

Many specialists in the field of child sexual abuse have concluded that it is rare for individuals to fabricate accusations of these crimes. In 2002, the *New York Times* interviewed Patrick Schiltz, former associate dean of the University of St. Thomas law school in [St. Paul,] Minnesota and now a Federal judge, who had defended Catholic dioceses against sexual-abuse lawsuits in more than 500 cases. Judge Schiltz expressed the belief that "fewer than 10" of those cases were based on false accusations.

Likewise, I have spoken with scores of men and women who claim to have been sexually abused. I also have concluded that the overwhelming majority are telling the truth and, of all the victims I have interviewed, I am not aware of a single abuser who has been indicted for his or her alleged abuse.

After determining the authenticity of that Customs report, I started to investigate a second pedophile network that reportedly had been sheltered by entities within Federal law enforcement. It was then that I truly entered a parallel universe that encompasses the refined destruction of children along with its cover-up by the very state and Federal authorities who have pledged to protect them from the depravity of evil

Swept Under the Rug

Hierarchical organizations such as the Catholic Church and the Boy Scouts have come under fire for covering up or failing to appropriately deal with the sexual abuse of children. But it's not just organizations like Penn State that turn a blind eye, [president and chief executive officer of the Child Abuse Prevention Association Jeanetta] Issa said. Families frequently deny child abuse in their midst too, Issa told *LiveScience* in November [2011]. In one case Issa was familiar with, an adult woman who had been sexually abused by her brother throughout her youth began to see signs that her niece might have become his next victim. The woman finally spoke out.

"In her whole family, nobody believed her," Issa said. "They tried to have her committed to a mental hospital."

Stephanie Pappas, LiveScience, July 12, 2012.
www.livescience.com.

men—a universe where lies masquerade as truth, shadows reflect light, and innocence is condemned.

Perpetrators Freed, Victims Indicted

I spent the next seven years researching and writing a book documenting a nationwide pedophile ring that pandered children to a cabal of men with power and prestige. The ring's pimps were a pair of political powerbrokers who used a distinguished orphanage as a pedophilic reservoir. With access to thousands of documents that were sealed by two grand juries, as well as the sealed testimony of one, I demonstrated that state and Federal grand jury processes in Nebraska played an integral role in the cover-up.

Instead of indicting the alleged perpetrators, these grand juries indicted the victims who would not recant their accounts of abuse on charges of perjury. In one case, a 21-year-old who had been abused since adolescence was indicted on eight counts of perjury by both state and Federal grand juries. Facing more than 300 years in prison, she still refused to recant. Her travesty of a trial resulted in a prison sentence of nine to 15 years. She spent nearly two years in solitary confinement.

This individual was released from prison in 2000, and she has become a model citizen: she is happily married and gainfully employed. Conversely, one of the ring's pedophilic pimps, who was not charged with a single count of child abuse, moved halfway across the country. By 2009, he had enmeshed himself among a new brood of economically disadvantaged children.

Refusals to Publish

Before the book came into print, I attempted to publish an article on the subject matter. After I felt I had collected clear proof of the child abuse and its cover-up, I distilled the information into an article and submitted it to numerous mainstream magazines, but none would go with it. The magazine editors rejected it without even looking at the thousands of pages of corroborating law enforcement and social services documentation I had collected. Although I was put off by the editors' apparent callousness or perhaps fear for their careers, I thought the main problem may have been that I shoehorned such a sprawling story into an article.

Undeterred, I wrote a rather lengthy book proposal and gave it to the major literary agency representing me. Within weeks, I was dumped as a client. Still determined, I found a second agent who tried to sell the book proposal, but he found no takers. I did meet with one publisher, however, his primary concern was any potential libel action, not the destruction of numerous children. Finally, I found a small publisher on the West Coast who had the fortitude to publish my book, which, in addition to more than 500 pages of narrative, provides 100 pages of documentation, but no one in the mainstream media would review or even mention it. I managed to get copies to the producers for television personalities who are child-welfare advocates, and they would not touch the story, either.

Fear, Disbelief, and Misplaced Loyalty

Possibly, most media were scared off by the fact that two grand juries declared that the perpetrators had not abused a single child and a jury had found the young woman guilty of fabricating her story and convicted her of perjury. Juries, after all, are the finders of fact in our system, but it also is true that her charges and those of the other victims implicated some very powerful figures. I also believe that many editors looking at the summary concluded that my tale could not possibly be true, and there was no reason to even look at the book.

These circumstances, though, are quite different from what we know of the situation at Penn State. If the Sandusky allegations are true,[1] I would guess that his leverage there was the potential besmirching of the reputations of Penn State and his coaching associates. Penn State has prestige, and rightly so. It has done a lot of good. Institutions, however well-intentioned, are made up of individuals. Pedophilic predators are attracted to environments full of prey: schools, churches, youth groups, etc. The mandate of these institutions must be to protect the children in their charge, and to put that imperative ahead of the protection of their own reputations.

Indeed, Penn State has refused to release records from its 1998 inquiry involving Sandusky, and the state's Office of Open Records recently upheld its decision. The school's re-

---

1. Sandusky was convicted in 2012 and sentenced to sixty years in prison. Penn State's president was forced to resign, and the head football coach (college football coaching legend Joe Paterno) and the athletic director were fired.

fusal to release these records certainly suggests it still is putting its reputation ahead of the alleged victims when common decency demands transparency at this point.

The Perfect Recipe for Cover-up

Another factor that dooms many investigations, and abets corrupt ones, is that victims frequently are from disadvantaged backgrounds, and the adult luring the child frequently introduces the underage individual to drugs or alcohol, further eroding that victim's credibility. Moreover, the abuser often has powerful allies in law enforcement, government, and the media, who decide that the sordid details are too hot to handle. Add into the mix the public's understandable squeamishness toward the entire subject of pedophilia, and we arrive at the perfect recipe for cover-up.

The reality is that many perpetrators are not shady men in dirty, threadbare trench coats living in seedy hotels, but are, in fact, pillars of our community. Until our society addresses these facts and its institutions are willing to face embarrassment, instead of heaping more abuse upon victims, our national shame of rampant child abuse and its cover-up are unlikely to end.

> "Schools—and the government agency that oversees them—[have failed] to prevent assaults and then to resolve these cases."

Colleges Insufficiently Respond to Campus Sexual Assaults

Joseph Shapiro

In the following viewpoint, National Public Radio (NPR) investigative reporter Joseph Shapiro presents the common weaknesses in colleges' responses to sexual assaults on their campuses. When victims report assaults, he says, punishment for assailants tends to be light, if there is punishment at all, and it is often victims who end up leaving, not perpetrators. Despite the 1990 passage of the Clery Act, some schools continue to underreport or even to cover up sexual assaults. While colleges are generally improving in terms of preventing sexual assault, Shapiro contends, they still do not respond strongly enough when it does happen.

As you read, consider the following questions:

1. According to Laura Dunn's professor, as cited by Shapiro, what percentage of rape victims do not report their being assaulted?

Joseph Shapiro, "Campus Rape Victims: A Struggle for Justice," *Morning Edition*, February 24, 2010. Copyright © 2010 by NPR. All rights reserved. Republished with permission.

2. As reported by Shapiro, what does the Clery Act require colleges to do?

3. What was the Department of Education's finding in Laura Dunn's case, according to the author?

A college campus isn't the first place that comes to mind in a discussion about violent crime.

But research funded by the U.S. Department of Justice estimates that 1 out of 5 college women will be sexually assaulted. NPR's [National Public Radio's] investigative unit teamed up with journalists at the Center for Public Integrity (CPI) to look at the failure of schools—and the government agency that oversees them—to prevent these assaults and then to resolve these cases.

A Hidden Attack

When a woman is sexually assaulted on a college campus, her most common reaction is to keep it quiet. Laura Dunn says she stayed quiet about what happened in April 2004 at the end of her freshman year at the University of Wisconsin.

"I always thought that rape was when someone got attacked by a stranger and you had to fight back," she says.

That night, Dunn was drinking so many raspberry vodkas that they cut her off at a frat house party. Still, she knew and trusted the two men who took her back to a house for what she thought was a quick stop before the next party. Instead, she says they raped her as she passed in and out of consciousness.

For a long time, she had a hard time even letting herself call it a rape. It just didn't make sense with the way she saw her life. For one thing, she had a boyfriend she had been dating for four years.

"We were getting close to marriage. We'd been waiting together, so I was still a virgin, and it just didn't fit what I'd wanted my life to be and what I'd planned out my life to be," says Dunn. "So I just kind of pushed it to the side, said, you know, it's this bad incident that happened, and it was just a mistake, we were all drunk. And I just chose to, like, put it there."

Deciding to Act

Instead, Dunn focused on her schoolwork and kept her grades up. But she couldn't sleep. She lost weight. She broke up with her boyfriend, without ever telling him about the attack.

And she didn't report it.

Fifteen months later, she was sitting in class. The professor was talking about how, in wartime, rape is used as a weapon of terror. "And this professor, who I'll forever respect, stopped the lecture and said, 'You know, I want to talk about rape on this campus.'"

The professor said that more than 80 percent of victims stay silent.

"And she said, 'I want you to know this has happened in my class to my students, and there is something you can do about it, and there is someone you can talk about it with.' And she told me about the dean of students." And with that, Dunn made a decision. "I know it was rape, and now I know that there's something I can do about it. And so the moment that lecture let up, I walked across to the dean of students' office and I reported that day."

Going Public

Colleges and universities got their current-day responsibility to investigate and prevent sexual assaults as a result of an April 1986 crime, after a hard-fought advocacy campaign by the family of Jeanne Clery.

"What happened to Jeanne was so amazingly unreal," her mother, Connie Clery, says. "She was in the right place where she should have been—in her own bed in the dorm at 6 o'clock in the morning, fast asleep. There were three automatically locking doors that should have been locked, which she thought were locked, and she didn't have an enemy in the world. And Lehigh was such a safe-looking place, you know?"

Jeanne Clery was 19 and a freshman at Lehigh University. A stranger—he was a student—raped, tortured and strangled her.

In their grief, Connie Clery and her husband devoted the rest of their lives to making college campuses safer. "So if it happened to Jeanne, it could certainly happen to somebody else," Connie Clery says from the dining room of her home overlooking the St. Lucie River in Florida. "That's why I decided I had to do something to save others from such a horror."

Connie's husband, Howard, sold his successful business to underwrite their work. Connie, who had been terrified of speaking in public, went on TV morning shows and testified before lawmakers.

Public Scrutiny Produced Safer Campuses

Their idea was simple: Force schools to disclose all crime that happens on campus. Then students—and their parents—would be informed. That would make the campus safer because faced with public scrutiny, college presidents would have no choice but to get serious about preventing crime.

Twenty years ago [in 1990], Congress passed that disclosure law, now known as the Jeanne Clery Act.

There's been success. Over a recent 10-year period [1994–2004], the U.S. Department of Justice says campuses have reported a 9 percent drop in violent crime and a 30 percent drop in property crime, according to S. Daniel Carter, the public policy director of Security on Campus Inc., the nonprofit group started by the Clerys.

Carter points to another indicator of change: a 5 percent increase in campus police pay, adjusted for inflation. He says that shows that "the Clery Act really has led to colleges and universities to take campus security and protecting their students more seriously than they did 20 years ago."

But Carter says there have been shortcomings, too. And Connie Clery agrees. "The Department of Education has been a disappointment to me," she says.

A Question of Enforcement

The federal Department of Education regulates schools under the Clery Act. But it has fined offending schools just six times. Most fines have been small. The biggest—for $350,000—came against Eastern Michigan University. Administrators there covered up the 2006 rape and murder of a student, 22-year-old Laura Dickinson, letting her parents think she'd died suddenly of natural causes.

The Department of Education can also hold schools accountable under Title IX of the Education Amendments of 1972. Title IX is best known as the federal civil rights law that requires equality in men's and women's sports teams. But the law is broader than that. It says that any educational institution that takes federal funding cannot discriminate against women. Sexual harassment, sexual assault and rape are also considered discrimination on the basis of sex.

"All too often, victims are revictimized by being forced to encounter their assailants on campus day in and day out," says Carter, "especially if they are suffering from some sort of post-traumatic stress, which can trigger panic attacks and have a significant adverse impact on their ability to continue their educational program."

Few Repercussions

Title IX is among the strongest tools for enforcement at the Education Department, says Carter. But few women know to use it. And when they do, the department rarely acts. Between 1998 and 2008, the department ruled against just five universities out of 24 complaints. That's according to records obtained through the Freedom of Information Act by the Center for Public Integrity. No punishment was given in those cases—simply guidance on how to improve campus procedures.

Presented with those findings, Russlynn Ali, the Education Department's assistant secretary for civil rights, says her office is stepping up outreach to students and assistance to schools. "We want them to get training, we want to provide some help," she says, "so that the adults and the students alike can ensure that this plague—it's really has become a plague in this country—begins to diminish."

Ali says she's willing to take steps not used by her predecessors: to withdraw federal funding from offending schools and refer cases to the Department of Justice for possible prosecution.

A Failed Last Resort

In Laura Dunn's case, by the time she reported to campus officials, one of the men she accused had graduated. The other said the sex was consensual. The University of Wisconsin took nine months to investigate, then decided against punishment.

As a last resort, Dunn asked the Department of Education to find that the university had failed in its responsibility to act promptly and to end the sexual harassment she faced being on campus with her alleged attacker.

Two years after Dunn graduated from the university, and nearly four years after the incident, a thick document came in the mail to her apartment. It was the finding by the Department of Education, dated August 6, 2008. She flipped to the last page. "I went straight to the conclusion," she explains.

It said the University of Wisconsin—despite taking nine months on her case—had acted properly. Defeated, Dunn didn't read on. She threw the papers on the top of a pile of other documents in the corner of her bedroom.

"You know, I could have fought it again, and I could have appealed. But that would have meant I would have had to read it, and at that point in my life, just reading it, I just didn't even want to. I did not want to read the ugly things that people said."

But Laura Dunn is no longer silent. She's a leader in a national grass-roots campaign, called PAVE [Promoting Awareness, Victim Empowerment], to get rape survivors to speak out in public.

He Said, She Said

Kevin Helmkamp, the associate dean of students at the University of Wisconsin, said privacy rules prohibited him from speaking specifically about Dunn's case. But he said the university investigates each allegation carefully, and provides support and resources to students.

Last September [2009], the university updated its rules on student conduct. In the past, the school required "clear and convincing evidence" to find an accused student responsible of a sexual assault. But now, in line with most other schools as well as with federal guidelines, the standard is the lower "preponderance of evidence."

"Mathematically, that would be 51 percent of evidence," Helmkamp says, although in fact, the judgment is more subjective.

Sexual assault cases are among the most difficult matters to determine, he says. "They clearly are very, very difficult cases to investigate. Usually, there is not a lot of corroborating evidence for one side or the other," he says. "It does tend to come down to one person saying this happened and the other person saying, no it didn't happen that way." The result, "I can assure you, is that someone is going to be unhappy" with the outcome of a decision.

Prevention, Not Punishment

Campus disciplinary programs are not set up like a court of law. Officials lack subpoena power and often end up with the accused and the accuser telling their stories, with a panel of a

The Rights of Sexual Assault Victims

What's now called the Clery Act, enacted in November 1990, requires that higher education institutions publicly disclose all crime that happens on campus. The idea was that students and their parents should be informed—and that public scrutiny would force colleges to get serious about preventing crime.

A 1992 amendment to the Clery Act added a victims' bill of rights, which requires schools to provide certain basic rights to survivors of sexual assaults on campus, including:

Giving the alleged victim and the alleged assailant equal opportunity to have others present in disciplinary proceedings.

Notifying alleged victims of their right to pursue justice through local police, and of the availability of counseling services.

Notifying alleged victims that they have the option of changing classes and dormitory assignments in order to avoid their alleged assailants.

If a university fails to appropriately handle a reported case of sexual assault, alleged victims can report this to the U.S. Department of Education. Under Title IX of the Education Amendments of 1972—a civil rights law that prohibits sex-based discrimination—sexual harassment, sexual assault and rape are also considered discrimination on the basis of sex.

Joseph Shapiro, National Public Radio, February 24, 2010.

few campus officials trying to figure out the truth. Schools see the role of these courts [as being] to teach students more than to mete out justice. That's also why punishments tend to be light: Counseling and alcohol treatment are more likely than expulsion. The result is that large numbers of women who say they've been assaulted feel dissatisfied with the results, and large numbers of women end up leaving school.

Sometimes there are false accusations—although studies on college campuses in the U.S. and Great Britain show those are rare: about 3 to 6 percent of cases.

Because it's hard to sort out truth in such cases, more school administrators are realizing the importance of putting more emphasis on prevention.

Acknowledging Efforts at UCLA

Earlier this month [February 2010], Security on Campus, the group started by Connie and Howard Clery, presented its annual security award to Nancy Greenstein. She's with the campus police department at UCLA [University of California at Los Angeles].

That university, in its annual Clery report, shows more sexual assaults than many other schools the same size. At first, that makes it seem like UCLA is unsafe. But Carter says Greenstein was honored for creating a place where women feel comfortable going to police, and so more of them come forward to report a sexual assault.

Greenstein says the campus police, administration and student groups have increased efforts at prevention. And one of the most effective programs gets students talking to other students about the risks of drinking and rape, and the meaning of consent.

"You don't want any students to be harmed," she says of sexual assault. "It changes people's lives. So many students who have been victimized, in a sense they're never the same. And if we can prevent that from happening ... if I can prevent one person from being victimized, then that's successful."

"[Sexual assault] is not a problem that we are going to ignore in the United States military."

The US Military Is Now Taking Sexual Assault Seriously

Leon E. Panetta

Leon E. Panetta was the United States Secretary of Defense from 2011 to 2013. In this viewpoint, Panetta explains the steps taken by the Department of Defense (DoD) to address the problem of sexual assault in the US military. The DoD, he reports, has improved its system for collecting and tracking sexual assault reports, changed procedures to encourage reporting and take reports more seriously, improved the quality of investigations, strengthened penalties for perpetrators, and expanded efforts to educate service members about military sexual assault policy and procedures.

As you read, consider the following questions:

1. What does Panetta say will be the minimum action required of a local unit commander in response to a sexual assault report after the new directive is put into place?

Leon E. Panetta, "Secretary Panetta Remarks on Capital Hill," US Department of Defense, April 17, 2012.

2. What did the DoD set up to improve evidence collection in sexual assault cases, according to Panetta?

3. According to the new policy Panetta describes, in what timeframe will new service members need to be briefed on the DoD's sexual assault policy

Sexual assault has no place in the military. It is a violation of everything that the U.S. military stands for. [Chairman of the Joint Chiefs of Staff] General [Martin E.] Dempsey and I have, I think, made it a point to try to open up the military to everyone who wants to serve this country, and the problem is that sexual assault remains a disincentive for many to become a part of the United States military. We've got to deal with that and we will.

We have taken some steps in the past to try to begin to deal with this problem. We have put forward a number of initiatives. And let me just summarize some of the past issues that we've done. We've assigned a two-star general as the director of the sexual assault prevention and response office to try to highlight the importance of dealing with this issue and increase the command authority in dealing with this issue.

We've implemented a number of new policies that expand legal assistance, that expedite transfers for those that want to move from units, and that also provide extended document retention, something that was not the case in the past. We also have stood up a DoD [Department of Defense]-wide 24/7 anonymous hotline to be able to encourage victims to report. And in addition to that we've now activated an integrated database that contains all the information with regards to sexual assault.

Moving Forward

We need to do more and I've made a commitment that we will move forward to incorporate some of the ideas that have been suggested by members of Congress into additional steps here. We believe that we've developed a set of initiatives that fundamentally change the way the department deals with this problem. Let me summarize some of the steps that we're recommending and that we will work with Congress in trying to include in our legislative package.

First of all, as of the next few days what I will do is change the way these cases are handled in the military. I intend to enter a directive as secretary of defense that will elevate the disposition of sexual assault cases so that at a minimum these cases are disposed of at a special court martial level. That means that the local unit commander is required to report these cases, any sexual assault case, is required to report that to a special court martial level, generally a colonel status, or if necessary to a general court martial level for investigation into the matter to be handled.

And the key here is that at the local unit level sometimes these matters are put aside, they're not followed up with. This requires that any time a complaint is received that it is referred up the chain of command for action. It ensures that we emphasize the role of the chain of command and that we continue to emphasize that all commanders have to exercise good discipline, take control, and they need to understand that everyone has responsibility to deal with these issues. But most importantly we are assured that at a higher command level we will have action taken with regards to the complaints that have been made.

Using Personnel Wisely

Secondly, to be able to effectively investigate and prosecute these sexual assault cases it requires a particular expertise in gathering the evidence. We are creating a special victims unit or capability within each of the services to be able to do this. This will ensure that we have highly trained experts who are trained in evidence collection, the best way to interview survi-

An Upward Trend in Reporting Assaults

Number of service members victims in reports of sexual assault to Department of Defense authorities (unrestricted and restricted) for fiscal years (FY) 2007 through 2011.

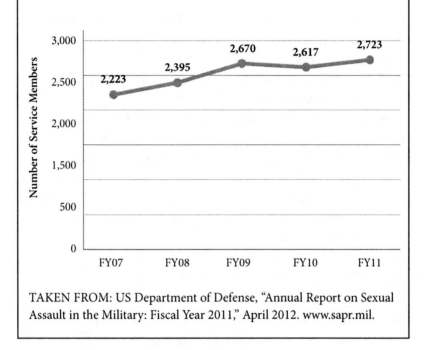

TAKEN FROM: US Department of Defense, "Annual Report on Sexual Assault in the Military: Fiscal Year 2011," April 2012. www.sapr.mil.

vors of the sexual assault, and who have [insight into] offender behavior in being able to determine what those behaviors are like.

We also want to ensure that members of the National Guard and Reserve who file complaints are able to remain on active duty once they've filed those complaints in order to ensure that their sexual assault complaint is handled. At the present time, those in the Guard and Reserve, if they're on active duty and make a complaint, they then are moved into their National Guard or Reserve status and they lose the ability to continue that kind of prosecution of their complaint.

What we're doing is requiring that they be able to stay on active duty in order to ensure that the case is continuing to be handled.

Educate and Provide New Resources

And fourthly, we have to do everything we can to train and educate the force with regards to these issues. We're going to focus on the newest members, new arrivals, and require that DoD sexual assault policy be explained and briefed to them within 14 days of entering active duty.

Secondly, we also want a mandate that information on sexual assault sources such as the DoD self-help line and other things are widely publicized so that members are aware of what's available to them. And thirdly, we are looking to require commanders to conduct annual climate assessment analysis with regards to sexual assault, something that isn't required at the present time.

The Need to Be Sensitive to the Issue

This is a strong package essential to being able to prevent and respond to the crime of sexual assault. There's no silver bullet when it comes to this issue but what is required is that everyone from the secretary to the chairman of the joint chiefs all the way down at every command level be sensitive to this issue, be aware to take their responsibility to take action on these cases.

The most important thing we can do is prosecute the offenders, deal with those that have broken the law and committed this crime. And if we can do that then we can begin to deal with this issue—not only prosecute those that are involved, but more importantly send a signal that this is not—this is not a problem that we are going to ignore in the United States military.

"[The military is] charging more and more people with bogus [sexual assault] cases just to show that they do take it seriously."

The US Military Is Prosecuting Questionable Sexual Assault Cases to Improve Its Image

Marisa Taylor and Chris Adams

In the following viewpoint, Marisa Taylor and Chris Adams, national investigative reporters for McClatchy Newspapers, explain that the Department of Defense has put into place new policies and procedures after widespread reports that it was turning a blind eye to sexual assault within its ranks. However, the authors say, the military is now prosecuting cases that are so lacking in support that they would not even go to trial in a civilian court. Aside from resulting in wrongful convictions, many say that this strategy has actually backfired, so that sexual assault cases are taken less seriously than they were before.

Marisa Taylor and Chris Adams, "Military's Newly Aggressive Rape Prosecution Has Own Pitfalls," *McClatchy DC*, November 28, 2011. Reproduced by permission.

As you read, consider the following questions:

1. By what percentage did the number of court-martialed sexual assault cases increase between 2009 and 2010, according to Taylor and Adams?

2. Who decides whether to press charges in the military justice system, according to the authors?

3. On how many charges was Sergeant Jamie Walton indicted, as reported by Taylor and Adams?

By the time Marine Staff Sgt. Jamie Walton went to trial on rape charges, his accuser had changed her story several times.

A military lawyer who evaluated the case told Walton's commander they didn't have enough evidence to go to trial on sexual assault charges. The prosecutor even agreed. But the Marines ignored the advice.

"Everyone knew I didn't rape her," said Walton, who was acquitted of the charge last year [2010]. "But they went ahead with the trial anyway."

Walton's questionable prosecution clashes with the public's perception of a soft-on-rape military. A McClatchy analysis found that the military is prosecuting a growing number of rape and sexual assault allegations, including highly contested cases that would be unlikely to go to trial in many civilian courts.

However, most of the accused aren't being convicted of serious crimes. Such results are provoking cynicism within the armed forces that the politics of rape are tainting a military justice system that's as old as the country itself.

A Shift in Approach

"In the media and on Capital Hill, there's this myth that the military doesn't take sexual assault seriously," said Michael Waddington, a former Army judge advocate who now defends the cases. "But the reality is they're charging more and more people with bogus cases just to show that they do take it seriously."

McClatchy's review of nearly 4,000 sexual assault allegations demonstrates that the military has taken a more aggressive stance. Last year [2010], military commanders sent about 70 percent more cases to courts-martial that started as rape or aggravated sexual-assault allegations than they did in 2009.

However, only 27 percent of the defendants were convicted of those offenses or other serious crimes in 2009 and 2010, McClatchy found after reviewing the cases detailed in the Defense Department's annual sexual assault reports. When factoring in convictions for lesser offenses—such as adultery, which is illegal in the military, or perjury—about half the cases ended in convictions.

The military's conviction rate for all crimes is more than 90 percent, according to a 2010 report to Congress by the Pentagon.

"The pendulum has swung," said Victor Kelley, a former federal prosecutor who's a defense attorney with the law firm National Military Justice Group. "It may be true that years ago some of these allegations weren't given the attention they deserved. But now many of them are given more deference than they're due."

The Difficulties of Prosecution

But legal officials with all four military branches say the low conviction rate shows how difficult it is to convict the suspects, not that innocent people are being sent to trial. One common problem in all courts—military and civilian alike—is that a sexual assault victim's behavior comes under attack as much as that of the accused does. As a result, juries may not convict despite hearing significant evidence that a rape occurred.

Making acquittals even more likely, the military is prosecuting more contested cases under a controversial law that broadens the definition of sexual assault. Under the 2006 law, the military can argue that a victim was sexually assaulted because she was "substantially incapacitated" from excessive drinking and couldn't have consented.

"What would you have us do? Tell the victim she can't get justice just because it's a hard case?" asked Timothy MacDonnell, an Army prosecutor who retired in 2008. "Then you're saying to sexual predators, 'Just be careful and make sure you do it in private and you'll get away with it.'"

A Different System

In dozens of interviews, however, a wide range of people who are involved in the military justice system questioned whether the military was weighing the proper legal considerations when deciding whether to take criminal action.

Unlike in the civilian justice system, a military commander, not a prosecutor, makes the final call on whether to press charges. At times, the commanders disregard their legal advisers' recommendations and pursue allegations of sexual assault, raising concerns that the anti-rape campaign of advocacy groups and Congress is influencing them.

Even some prosecutors say the strategy has backfired, making it more difficult to crack down on the crime in general.

"Because there is this spin-up of 'We have to take cases seriously even though they're crap,' it creates a kind of a climate of blasé attitudes," said one Navy prosecutor, who asked to remain anonymous because she feared retaliation for speaking out.

"There is a pressure to prosecute, prosecute, prosecute. When you get one that's actually real, there's a lot of skepticism. You hear it routinely: 'Is this a rape case or is this a Navy rape case?'"

Some Assaults Still Go Unpunished

The reality, of course, is many women and men are raped or sexually assaulted in the military. When confronted with the crime even now, some commanders aren't aggressive enough in cracking down, many from all perspectives agree.

North Carolina native Stephanie Schroeder, for instance, said her superiors were unsympathetic after a fellow Marine followed her into a women's bathroom and raped her.

Her superior said, "'Don't come bitching to me because you had sex and changed your mind,'" recalled Schroeder, who's since joined a lawsuit alleging that the military failed to protect her from the 2002 assault.

Her attacker was never punished, Schroeder said, while she was disciplined after her commanders concluded that she'd lied.

A federal judge is expected to decide soon whether to give Schroeder and others class action status in suing the military.

But many military attorneys describe cases such as Schroeder's as isolated instances that garner most of the attention and outrage.

"Even with this spotlight shining on the military, it has not eliminated the horror story of some commander ignoring valid charges," said Dwight Sullivan, senior appellate defense counsel for the Air Force. "We haven't prevented the horror stories and now we've created another problem of overcharging."

Increased Pressure to Prosecute

The pressure ratcheted up in 2003, when female cadets at the Air Force Academy accused commanders of ignoring their sexual assaults. In the wake of the scandal, the military prosecuted several of the accused.

The cases didn't go well. One of the juries took only 20 minutes in 2006 to acquit a defendant. After a judge dismissed charges against another cadet, civilian prosecutors declined to charge him in 2007 because of a lack of evidence.

In fact, none of the men accused in the scandal were convicted of charges related to non-consensual sex, said attorneys who were involved.

Citing such failures, Congress boosted the military's anti-sexual assault budget and crafted the new law to help prosecute cases.

As lawmakers turned up the pressure, the military acted on the demands. The number of all sex-crime allegations sent to courts-martial increased from 113 in 2004 to 532 in 2010, according to Defense Department data.

Too often, however, defendants are being prosecuted despite qualms about the evidence, attorneys said.

Questionable Allegations

In Walton's case, the accuser initially denied having sex with him when her commander questioned her.

After Walton confessed to adultery and urged her to tell the truth, she admitted having an affair with him. At that point, she said in a sworn statement that she and Walton had picked up "protection" before heading to a hotel. She denied drinking any alcohol.

Three months later, she changed her account again, saying Walton had plied her with hard liquor before taking her to the hotel. While they were watching TV on the bed, she said, "he all of a sudden rolled on top of me."

"I don't think I said anything," she said in a statement. "I just remember my clothes coming off and I accepted it was happening."

The woman said she realized she'd been raped after attending anti-sexual assault classes. She notified the lawyer who was defending her against adultery charges. The woman also told her estranged husband.

Military Sexual Assault Cases

Data on sexual assault allegations in the US Military in 2009–2010 show a low conviction rate.

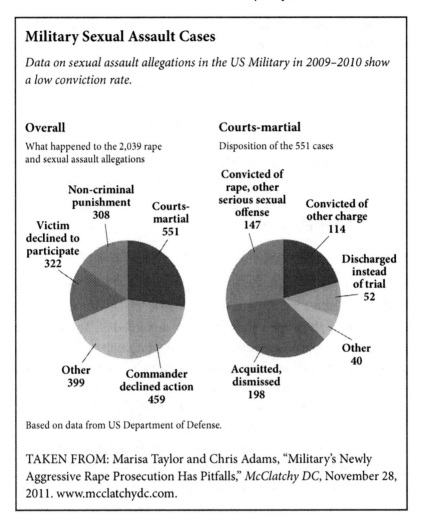

Overall

What happened to the 2,039 rape and sexual assault allegations

Non-criminal punishment 308

Victim declined to participate 322

Courts-martial 551

Other 399

Commander declined action 459

Courts-martial

Disposition of the 551 cases

Convicted of rape, other serious sexual offense 147

Convicted of other charge 114

Discharged instead of trial 52

Other 40

Acquitted, dismissed 198

Based on data from US Department of Defense.

TAKEN FROM: Marisa Taylor and Chris Adams, "Military's Newly Aggressive Rape Prosecution Has Pitfalls," *McClatchy DC*, November 28, 2011. www.mcclatchydc.com.

Rejecting Legal Advice

When a military lawyer, known as an investigating officer, reviewed her allegations, he recommended that the Marines drop the aggravated sexual assault charge.

Not only had the accuser's story changed, friends said she'd told them the sex had been consensual and that she would do it again because she thought her husband was cheating on her.

The commander nonetheless rebuffed the lawyers' advice, pursuing nine charges against Walton that ranged from aggravated sexual assault to indecent language. Walton's possible fate changed from expulsion from the military to 30 years in prison.

"They threw everything at me to see what would stick," he said.

Commanders such as Walton's are instructed to consider the evidence, but they aren't required to follow their lawyers' advice. They also can weigh other interests such as the "good order and discipline" of their troops.

Validity of Accusations Tested at Trial

Given the push to prosecute, many commanders may see a trial as the best way to determine whether allegations are true.

"Most of the rape cases that I've defended in the military system never would have gone to trial in a civilian system because the prosecutor would say, 'There's no way I'm taking that to trial because I'm not going to get a conviction,'" said Charles Feldmann, a former military and civilian prosecutor who's now a defense attorney.

"But in the military, the decision-maker is an admiral or a general who is not going to put his career at risk on an iffy rape case by not prosecuting it. It's easy for him to say, 'Prosecute it.' If a jury acquits or convicts, then he can say justice was done either way."

"If a military commander dismisses a case and there's political backlash, he's going to take some real career heat over that dismissal," Feldmann said.

Success Rates Differ

Prosecutors outside the military appear to have more success at trial. There's no exact comparison with the civilian justice system, but a study of the nation's largest counties showed that 50 percent of the defendants charged with rape were found guilty of felonies in 2006, the most recent year for which those statistics are available. In New York state, almost 88 percent of the defendants charged with felony sex crimes were convicted in 2010.

In many civilian jurisdictions, the victim has to be unconscious or physically helpless or some sort of force would have to be used for prosecutors to proceed with sexual assault charges.

"A lot of the cases I help people with today I couldn't prosecute in my old jurisdiction because it's not criminalized by state law," said Teresa Scalzo, a veteran civilian prosecutor and the deputy director of the Navy's Trial Counsel Assistance Program.

Prosecutions Are No Less Difficult

While the 2006 law allows the military to pursue more sexual assault allegations, it didn't make the prosecution of such cases any easier, attorneys said.

In one recent case, an enlisted woman said she was drunk and fading in and out of consciousness when Army Spc. Kevin Olds touched her breast and put her hand on his penis. The pair had been drinking heavily together during a party. The woman, who was married, told a friend she "did not stop what was happening because she did not want to hurt (his) feelings," according to court records.

At one point, she said, "No, it's OK." That meant, she testified, that she didn't want him to be mad, but she did not want him to continue. She conceded that he may have misunderstood what she meant.

Olds, who was married as well, said he'd thought the woman had consented.

Earlier this year [2011], an investigating officer warned that "insufficient grounds" existed for a sexual assault prosecution.

A commander decided that charges should be pursued anyway. When the accuser said she'd prefer not to testify, the military sent the case to a summary court-martial, which is the equivalent of a misdemeanor court. Olds represented himself, and was acquitted on Nov. 15 [2011].

"It never should have seen the inside of a courtroom," said Charles Gittins, who represented Olds at the outset.

Policies Provide Incentives for Lying

Army Sgt. Derek Akins was supposed to go to trial earlier this year [2011] Fort Riley, Kan., after he was accused of sexually assaulting a fellow enlisted man's wife, according to court documents.

All three had been drinking heavily at a party at the couple's house. The husband said that he and his wife had shared a bottle of rum. The woman said Akins had flirted with her but that she didn't remember any sexual encounter because she'd passed out. The husband, however, contended that Akins had had sex with his semiconscious wife in his presence while all three were in the couple's bedroom.

In a last-minute reversal, the husband said that what had happened had been consensual. The military dropped the sexual assault charge.

"This is how nuanced and difficult these cases can be," said Philip Cave, Akins' lawyer and a retired Navy judge advocate. "The prosecution can be lied to as well."

In fact, an accuser and a defendant can have powerful motives to withhold important facts or lie about consensual sex. The military treats "fraternization"—socializing with someone who's lower in rank—as a crime. It's also illegal to have an extramarital affair or to have sex in some overseas locations.

The Significance of Due Process

McClatchy tried to talk to commanders about their roles in specific cases, but they either declined to be interviewed or referred a reporter to public affairs offices.

However, attorneys involved in prosecutions maintained that the military is weighing only the legal merits of cases, not the political ramifications.

"We have seen a push to prosecute more challenging cases," said Scalzo, who added that commanders "have become bolder because they've been educated about the nature of non-stranger sexual assault, especially when alcohol is involved."

Officials also denied that a low conviction rate signals any problems with the cases.

"I don't think it's an accurate way to measure the success of our program," said Janet Mansfield, an attorney with the Army's Office of the Judge Advocate General.

Asked how the Army was determining whether it's working, she responded that it was "hard to define."

"We want to see that due process exists," she said. "We want to see that victims are happy with the experience of the court-martial, if not the outcome."

Have the Scales Tipped Too Far?

Walton, however, thinks that the justice system has tilted unfairly in favor of the accuser.

After a two-year ordeal, the Marines convicted him of adultery and sent him to prison for six months. As soon as she made the rape accusation, the service dropped the adultery charge against his accuser. She was promoted, while he received a bad conduct discharge.

After 13 years in the military, Walton has lost his retirement and veteran's benefits, and the ability to attend college for free. And he worries that even an acquittal will be seen as a mark of guilt.

"A lot of people aren't going to like me because I made a stupid decision and I cheated on my wife," he said. "But I don't deserve to be seen as a rapist."

Periodical and Internet Sources Bibliography

The following articles have been selected to supplement the diverse views presented in this chapter.

Ginia Bellafante	"Revisionist History in Abuse Cases," *New York Times*, July 1, 2012.
Katrin Bennhold	"In Norway, Gender Equality Does Not Extend to the Bedroom," *New York Times*, October 24, 2011.
Nina Bernstein	"On Campus, a Law Enforcement System to Itself," *New York Times*, November 11, 2011.
Buzz Bissinger	"Penn State's New Villain," *Newsweek*, November 28, 2011.
The Economist	"Crime and Clarity: Rape Laws," September 1, 2012.
Malcolm Gladwell	"In Plain View," *New Yorker*, September 24, 2012.
Ashley Hayes	"Penn State and the Citadel: 'It's a Desire to Protect Their Own,'" *CNN Wire* (blog), November 15, 2011. http://news.blogs.cnn.com.
Melinda Hennenberger	"Sexual Assault on Campus: Lizzy's Ordeal," *National Catholic Reporter*, March 30, 2012.
Bill Keller	"Predators on Pedestals," *New York Times*, October 15, 2012.
James Risen	"Military Has Not Solved Problem of Sexual Assault, Women Say," *New York Times*, November 2, 2012.
Larry Wolff	"Free to Be a Sexual Predator?," *New York Times*, October 17, 2012.

CHAPTER 4

What Policies Can Help Reduce Sexual Violence?

Chapter Preface

When it comes to responding to sexual violence, the first institution in many people's minds is the US justice system. But in many sectors of society—including some with higher rates of sexual violence than the society as a whole—these crimes are often dealt with by separate, internal systems of justice. For instance, a report on sexual assault on college campuses by the Center for Public Integrity explains:

> Unlike criminal courts, which enforce rape statutes, college proceedings enforce "conduct codes" that list prohibited acts like "sexual assault" or "sexual contact." Their hearing boards operate under different procedural rules and evidence standards. Even their mission differs from the criminal justice system: Verdicts are educational, not punitive, opportunities.

The US military also has its own offices and procedures for handling reports of sexual assault.

There are valid justifications for having these separate systems of reporting and punishing sexual assaults. For example, they may be more knowledgeable about and attuned to the particularities of a subculture and its members. However, in recent years, several public cases have revealed the negative effects that such separate systems can have. Colleges across the United States have come under fire for everything from weak penalties to full cover-ups of sexual assault and sexual abuse. In 2007, the president and two other officials at Eastern Michigan University were fired for covering up the rape and murder of student Laura Dickinson in order to protect the university's reputation. In the infamous case of Penn State University, assistant football coach Jerry Sandusky's repeated sexual abuse and assault of underage boys was concealed by top university officials in order to preserve the reputation of its football program. The US military has also been criticized for failing to provide complete data on the number of sexual assaults in its ranks. According to some estimates, one in every three servicewomen is raped during her service. The Service Women's Action Networks reports that in 2011, "officials received 3,192 sexual assault reports. But only 1,518 of those reports led to referrals for possible disciplinary action, and only 191 military members were convicted at courts martial."

In response to public outcries regarding administrative cover-ups and ineffective penalties, many universities, the military, and other institutions have implemented new policies and procedures for dealing with reports of sexual abuse and assault. In 2005, the US Department of Defense (DoD) approved a new Sexual Assault Prevention and Response Policy, which, along with other changes, created the Sexual Assault Prevention and Response Office (SAPRO), a single point of authority and oversight for all branches of the military. While reporting is still too low, there was a 1 percent increase in reporting between 2010 and 2011. In April of 2011 SAPRO launched the DoD Safe Helpline, a 24/7 hotline resource for sexual assault victims, which had assisted more than 770 individuals by the end of that same year. In 2011, the US Department of Education's Office for Civil Rights sent a "Dear Colleague" letter to college administrators, clarifying and reiterating how sexual violence should be addressed on campuses under Title IX, the 1972 gender-equity law for educational institutions receiving federal funds. The letter outlined suitable time frames for the resolution of cases and the responsibilities of schools for supporting victims and improving campus environments. By September 2011, the office reports, at least twenty-five schools had already changed their sexual assault policies in response to the letter. If university and military hierarchies provide any indication, it seems likely that other public and private institutions will address weaknesses in their own policies and procedures in the near future. The viewpoints in this chapter describe policies and procedures that have been developed to help reduce sexual violence.

| "It should be for a court to decide—a civil court, not a whitewashing ecclesiastical court—whether the case against Ratzinger is as damning as it looks."

The Pope Should Be Prosecuted for Sexual Abuse Within the Church

Richard Dawkins

In the following viewpoint, British scientist, author, and celebrated atheist Richard Dawkins makes the case for legally prosecuting Pope Benedict XVI (who has since resigned from the papacy) for the pope's role in the cover-up of sex abuse by Catholic clergy. Dawkins calls attention to the pope's decision as the cardinal archbishop of Munich, Germany, not to defrock a priest who admitted to raping young boys, which the author claims is just more evidence that the pope values the church's public image over the welfare of children. Any government minister who made such a decision would be forced to resign and face legal repercussions, Dawkins asserts, and contends that the pope should suffer the same consequences.

Richard Dawkins, "The Pope Should Stand Trial," *The Guardian*, April 13, 2010. Copyright © 2010 by The Guardian. All rights reserved. Republished with permission.

As you read, consider the following questions:

1. Who have church spokesmen blamed for the sex abuse scandal, according to Dawkins?

2. In what way does the author's analogy between the pope and the British secretary of state for schools break down, by his own admission?

3. What is the headline involving himself that Dawkins corrects?

Sexual abuse of children is not unique to the Roman Catholic church, and Joseph Ratzinger [who became Pope Benedict XVI] is not one of those priests who raped altar boys while in a position of dominance and trust. But so often it is the subsequent cover-ups, even more than the original crimes, that do most to discredit an institution, and here the pope is in real trouble.

Pope Benedict XVI is the head of the institution as a whole, but we can't blame the present head for what was done before his watch. Except that in his particular case, as archbishop of Munich and as Cardinal Ratzinger, head of the Congregation for the Doctrine of the Faith (what used to be called the Inquisition), the very least you can say is that there is a case for him to answer. See, for example, three articles by my colleague Christopher Hitchens [in *Slate* magazine in 2010]. The latest smoking gun is the 1985 letter obtained by the Associated Press, signed by the then Cardinal Ratzinger to the diocese of Oakland about the case of Father Stephen Kiesle.

An Endless Stream of Excuses

Lashing out in desperation, church spokesmen are now blaming everybody but themselves for their current dire plight, which one official spokesman likens to the worst aspects of antisemitism (what are the best ones, I wonder?). Suggested culprits include the media, the Jews, and even Satan. The church is hiding behind a seemingly endless stream of excuses for having failed in its legal and moral obligation to report serious crimes to the appropriate civil authorities. But it was Cardinal Ratzinger's official responsibility to determine the church's response to allegations of child sex abuse, and his letter in the Kiesle case makes the real motivation devastatingly explicit. Here are his actual words, translated from the Latin in the AP [Associated Press] report:

> This court, although it regards the arguments presented in favour of removal in this case to be of grave significance, nevertheless deems it necessary to consider the good of the universal church together with that of the petitioner, and it is also unable to make light of the detriment that granting the dispensation can provoke with the community of Christ's faithful, particularly regarding the young age of the petitioner.

"The young age of the petitioner" refers to Kiesle, then aged 38, not the age of any of the boys he tied up and raped (11 and 13). It is completely clear that, together with a nod to the welfare of the "young" priest, Ratzinger's primary concern, and the reason he refused to unfrock Kiesle (who went on to re-offend) was "the good of the universal church".

The Priority of the Church's Image

This pattern of putting church PR [public relations] over and above the welfare of the children in its care (and what an understatement that is) is repeated over and over again in the cover-ups that are now coming to light, all over the world. And Ratzinger himself expressed it with damning clarity in this smoking gun letter.

In this case he was refusing the strong request of the local bishop that Kiesle should be unfrocked. Vatican standing orders were to refer such cases not to the civil authorities but to the church itself. The current campaign to call the church to

A Crime Under Any Law

[The pope] is not above or outside the law. He is the titular head of a small state. . . . This is a crime under any law (as well as a sin), and crime demands not sickly private ceremonies of "repentance," or faux compensation by means of church-financed payoffs, but justice and punishment. The secular authorities have been feeble for too long. . . . There has to be a reckoning, and it should start now.

Christopher Hitchens, Slate, March 29, 2010. www.slate.com.

account can take credit for the fact that this standing order has just changed, as of Monday 12 April 2010. Better late than never, as Galileo might have remarked in 1979, when the Vatican finally got around to a posthumous pardon.[1]

An Analogy of a Smaller Scale

Suppose the British secretary of state for schools received, from a local education authority, a reliable report of a teacher tying up his pupils and raping them. Imagine that, instead of turning the matter over to the police, he had simply moved the offender from school to school, where he repeatedly raped other children. That would be bad enough. But now suppose that he justified his decision in terms such as these:

Although I regard the arguments in favour of prosecution, presented by the local education authority, as of grave sig-

1. The Catholic Church accused physicist and astronomer Galileo Galilei (1564–1642) of heresy for promoting the sun-centered view of the solar system over the church-held earth-centered view. Pope John Paul II requested an in-depth study of the case in 1979, and the 1992 report noted the error of theologians' interpretations of Scripture in Galileo's time. Pope John Paul II acknowledged in 1992 that the Roman Catholic Church had erred in condemning Galileo for asserting that the earth revolves around the sun.

nificance, I nevertheless deem it necessary to consider the good of the government and the party, together with that of the offending teacher. And I am also unable to make light of the detriment that prosecuting the offender can provoke among voters, particularly regarding the young age of the offender.

The analogy breaks down, only in that we aren't talking about a single offending priest, but many thousands, all over the world.

The Pope Should Be Prosecuted

Why is the church allowed to get away with it, when any government minister who was caught writing such a letter would immediately have to resign in ignominy, and face prosecution himself? A religious leader, such as the pope, should be no different. That is why, along with Christopher Hitchens, I am supporting the current investigation of the pope's criminal complicity by Geoffrey Robertson QC [queen's counsel] and Mark Stephens. These excellent lawyers believe that, for a start, they have a persuasive case against the Vatican's status as a sovereign state, on the basis that it was just an ad hoc concoction driven by internal Italian politics under [twentieth-century Italian Fascist leader Benito] Mussolini, and was never given full status at the UN [United Nations]. If they succeed in this initial argument, the pope could not claim diplomatic immunity as a head of state, and could be arrested if he steps on British soil.

Why is anyone surprised, much less shocked, when Christopher Hitchens and I call for the prosecution of the pope, if he goes ahead with his proposed visit to Britain [which took place September 16–19, 2010, without incident]? The only strange thing about our proposal is that it had to come from us: where have the world's governments been all this time? Where is their moral fibre? Where is their commitment to treating everyone equally under the law? The UK [United

Kingdom] government, far from standing up for justice for the innocent victims of the Roman Catholic church, is preparing to welcome this grotesquely tainted man on an official visit to the UK so that he can "dispense moral guidance". Read that again: dispense moral guidance!

A Case for the Courts

Unfortunately I must end in bathos [a lapse into a more vulgar style], with a necessary correction of a damaging error in another newspaper. The *Sunday Times* of 11 April [2010], on its front page, printed the headline, "Richard Dawkins: I will arrest Pope Benedict XVI." This conjures up—as was doubtless intended—a ludicrous image of me ambushing the pontiff with a pair of handcuffs and marching him off in a half Nelson [a wrestling hold]. Blood out of a stone, but I finally managed to persuade that [Australian tycoon Rupert] Murdoch[-owned] paper to change the headline in the online edition.

Never mind headlines invented by foolish sub-editors, we are serious. It should be for a court to decide—a civil court, not a whitewashing ecclesiastical court—whether the case against Ratzinger is as damning as it looks. If he is innocent, let him have the opportunity to demonstrate it in court. If he is guilty, let him face justice. Just like anybody else.

> *"The very suggestion . . . of vicarious liability for the pope and other top Vatican officials indicates a complete lack of understanding about the structure of the Catholic Church."*

Accusing Pope Benedict

Ronald J. Rychlak

Ronald J. Rychlak is a professor of law at the University of Mississippi and an adviser to the Vatican's Permanent Observer Mission to the United Nations. In the following viewpoint, he addresses the petition accusing Pope Benedict XVI and three other Vatican officials of "crimes against humanity" filed by the Survivors Network of those Abused by Priests (SNAP) to the International Criminal Court (ICC). Rychlak argues that the petition does not meet the basic criteria for ICC cases, lacks evidence to support its charges, and is nothing more than a publicity stunt intended to damage the pope's reputation. (Pope Benedict XVI resigned on February 28, 2013.)

As you read, consider the following questions:

1. How does the ICC differ from the International Court of Justice, according to Rychlak?

Ronald J. Rychlak, "Accusing Pope Benedict," *National Review*, September 28, 2011. Copyright © 2011 by the National Review. All rights reserved. Republished with permission.

2. According to a SNAP spokesman cited by the author, what is the group's objective in filing the petition?

3. How does the author believe the ICC will respond to SNAP's petition?

Should Pope Benedict XVI be arrested?

That's what an advocacy group called Survivors Network of those Abused by Priests (SNAP) is calling for. Just before the pope left Rome for a pastoral visit to his native Germany, SNAP filed a petition with the International Criminal Court accusing the pope, the Vatican secretary of state, and two other Vatican officials of "crimes against humanity" and urging prosecution at The Hague. The wholly unsubstantiated charge is that these men have enabled the sex crimes committed by Catholic priests over several decades.

The ICC is a fairly new institution in international law, having been established only in 2002. Unlike the International Court of Justice, which was established as the judicial arm of the United Nations and resolves disputes between nations, the ICC has jurisdiction over individuals who have committed the worst human-rights abuses—genocide, war crimes, and crimes against humanity—or who have waged a war of aggression.

The ICC was intended to eliminate politics and impunity in the international legal system and provide a legitimate forum for those cases in which, for example, an ousted tyrant might evade justice in domestic courts. In practice, however, the ICC is seen in some quarters as having become politicized. Just last year, the African Union released a paper complaining that virtually all of the court's activity was directed against leaders in that continent.

Possibly SNAP hoped the ICC would regard its petition as an opportunity to show that it is not just going after Third World leaders. Who knows? If that is so, SNAP has insulted the ICC's judicial and prosecutorial integrity. What we do know is that SNAP is using the court as an instrument to achieve its real purposes: to tarnish the pope's reputation and to ensure publicity for itself just by having a petition pending against him.

It is worthy of note that matters can be brought before the ICC in several ways: The court's prosecutor may decide to pursue a case on his own initiative; the U.N. Security Council may refer a case to the court; a nation may refer a case to the court; or a private party may petition the court to open an investigation. This petition process is very susceptible to politicization. Anyone can file a petition, and anyone can be the subject of one.

The ICC has received requests to consider about 9,000 cases in the nine years since it was founded, but it has opened only six investigations. Of those six, three were referred by nations, two were referred by the Security Council, and one was opened on the prosecutor's own initiative. The ICC has *never* proceeded on a case based upon a petition like the one filed by SNAP. As for the balance of the requests, some have received public notice in passing. A few—like the one from SNAP—have garnered the frenzied media attention that scandalous allegations tend to generate. Of course, media frenzy was exactly what SNAP wanted, and most media outlets dutifully and uncritically cooperated. The petition's allegations were taken at face value, and no searching media light was cast upon the motives or tactics of the petitioners.

If there had been some critical analysis, it would have shown that SNAP's petition never alleges that any of the four named individuals personally committed crimes against humanity. Their responsibility would have to be premised on some novel version of the theory of *respondeat superior*. Yet a SNAP spokesman said the organization's goal is to jail the pope, and "our long-term chances are excellent."

The very suggestion of that kind of vicarious liability for the pope and other top Vatican officials indicates a complete lack of understanding about the structure of the Catholic Church. The universality in matters of liturgy and doctrine provided by the Holy See's communion with the whole of the Church is a primary source of the Church's catholicity. However, diocesan bishops and religious superiors enjoy tremendous autonomy when it comes to day-to-day affairs and administration. The people at SNAP are well aware of this, but nevertheless exploit the myth of a centralized Vatican "politburo" style of authority in an attempt to justify their petition.

Issues of ecclesiastical structure aside, as a legal matter the allegations in SNAP's petition do not fit the ICC's jurisdictional mandate. For example, while rape can constitute a crime against humanity, it can only do so when committed as part of a widespread or systematic attack directed against a civilian population. No false rhetoric in SNAP's petition can compensate for the fact that neither the pope nor the other named Vatican officials are or have been involved in any "systematic attack" against a civilian population.

It is also worth noting that the ICC was designed to punish the "worst of the worst" perpetrators. With respect to sexual abuse, the evidence clearly demonstrates that such crimes were committed not only within the Catholic Church, but also within other religious and civic groups and school systems, and often at rates higher than those for priest offenders. That is no excuse for any of the perpetrators, but it eliminates the ICC as a proper forum for prosecuting them or their superiors. The ICC was not intended as a court in which to prosecute countless leaders of churches, civic institutions, and schools throughout the world.

One has the sense from their press statements that SNAP activists are not bothered by such niceties as the true purpose of the ICC or its jurisdictional mandate. The attorneys representing SNAP, however, work out of the Center for Constitutional Rights, and they cannot so easily be let off the hook.

Setting a High Legal Bar

The challenge for SNAP [Survivors Network of those Abused by Priests] and the CCR [Center for Constitutional Rights] will be to show that the ICC [International Criminal Court] has jurisdiction over the case. . . . The ICC was founded in 1998 for the purpose of trying individuals for war crimes such as genocide and crimes against humanity.

Experts say the matter of the Roman Catholic Church's responsibility for cases of child abuse is outside the remit of the ICC. "It's a publicity stunt, it's nothing more," says British attorney Neil Addison.

Jason Walsh, Christian Science Monitor, *September 15, 2011.*

Those attorneys *know* that their petition does not state a valid claim before the ICC, but they filed it anyway.

The CCR attorneys are misusing this new and fragile instrument of international law as a political tool—in other words, they are using it in precisely the way that the ICC, at its inception, was intended to avoid. Indeed, the filing of the petition itself was organized as a media event—the kickoff to a major "European tour," replete with SNAP and CCR press conferences in European capitals. The CCR attorneys are not acting as lawyers; they are facilitating a publicity stunt. That is shameful behavior that brings disrepute to the legal profession and, because the petition itself is fallacious, ultimately will not advance the interests of abuse victims.

I find the attorneys' actions particularly troubling because I worked on a case with the CCR years ago, and I considered Morty Stavis—one of the founders of the CCR and a lawyer active there from 1983 until his death in 1992—a friend.

Morty was too good a lawyer to play such games. The CCR would not be involved in something like this if Morty were still alive.

Notwithstanding the widespread media attention that SNAP's petition has received, it is little more than a political statement that abuses the international judicial process. In due course, it will be rejected by the ICC and end up in a dusty file drawer somewhere. Unfortunately for those maligned in it, however, it will already have achieved its real political purpose, which is to sully reputations and generate propaganda. This may serve SNAP's anti-Vatican agenda, but it does not assist abuse victims one bit.

> *"That so many people watched [sexual violence] and did nothing suggests that we not only need tougher enforcement of laws against sexual violence . . . we need better ways of incentivizing bystanders to give a damn."*

Punish the Onlookers

Wendy Murphy

In the following viewpoint, Wendy Murphy, a former child abuse and sex crimes prosecutor and the author of And Justice for Some, *argues that there should be legal ramifications for those who witness sexual violence but do not intervene. She makes specific reference to the 2009 gang rape of a California high school student that several bystanders failed to report for more than two hours. Murphy says that since it is clear that many people will not intervene in such cases unless there are negative consequences for not doing so, these must be put into place.*

As you read, consider the following questions:

1. Under what condition did police say they could arrest witnesses in the 2009 California gang rape case, as reported by the author?

Wendy Murphy, "Punish the Onlookers," *Newsweek*, October 30, 2009. Copyright © 2009 Newsweek Inc. All rights reserved. Reprinted by permission.

2. According to Murphy, what argument do civil libertarians make concerning laws that require witnesses of crimes to report them?

3. What risk does Murphy admit would come with encouraging witnesses to intervene in a crime?

In Northern California, four young men, ages 15 to 19, have been charged with rape and special circumstances that could put them behind bars for life for the alleged gang assault of a 15-year-old girl outside a high school. But what of the nearly two-dozen people, including adults, who watched the alleged gang rape last Saturday and did nothing?

This wasn't just a few people standing around watching a barroom brawl or consensual group sex. This was a group of folks finding entertainment value in human savagery.

Cops say more arrests are likely for some of the witnesses—for "aiding and abetting"—but only if they can prove some degree of active participation that somehow facilitated the crime. Those who only enjoyed the spectacle will face no charges, though nearby security guards who also reportedly did nothing can and should face civil lawsuits for negligence.

This is when I start to think we should stop claiming to be the most civilized nation on earth.

If two-dozen people can stand by and do nothing while a group of men forces a parade of penises and other objects inside a defenseless 15-year-old girl, there's a long list of words and phrases I can think of using—but *civilized* isn't among them.

Yet we have no laws in place to punish or deter such vicious passivity.

Oxymoronic as it might sound, "vicious passivity" is exactly what we're talking about. This wasn't just a few people standing around watching a barroom brawl or consensual group sex.

Crime Witnesses Must Speak Up

There is nothing wise about the monkeys among us who see and hear about the evil of sexual abuse of vulnerable children and fail to speak. How much more evidence do we need when it comes to the notion that sexual predators are deliberate about finding their way to environments and circumstances that fuel their sickness?

Charles Pascal, Toronto Star, *July 9, 2012.*

This was a group of folks finding entertainment value in human savagery.

Four animals (apologies to PETA activists for the insult) allegedly did things to a teenage girl that even the most hardened criminals don't do to each other behind bars. And while it's incomprehensible that not one of them had the capacity for a moment of decency, it's almost harder to understand how two-dozen people thought so little of the crime that not one of them did anything to help.

If this case is an expression of how some young men feel about sexuality and violence, it simply isn't practical anymore to expect people to treat each other with civility. And even if this case is an anomaly, one 15-year-old suffering the way this victim did is more than any society should tolerate.

That so many people watched and did nothing suggests that we not only need tougher enforcement of laws against sexual violence—only a small percentage of rapists spend even one day behind bars—we need better ways of incentivizing bystanders to give a damn. Put another way, it's embarrassing that doing nothing is OK, but without some legal ramification for such interpersonal inertia, doing nothing will always be the preferred path of least resistance for many people.

One case doesn't an epidemic make, but gang rape isn't exactly rare. It happens often enough that there's actually a pet name for it. "Running a Train" is what opportunistic rapists call it when they line up to get "f—ked," as one person reportedly described it to a bystander outside Richmond High. In short, it's about guys reveling in the fact that there's an incapacitated female body nearby to which a sex offender can do whatever he wants.

That one human being has the capacity to so mistreat another is not news. Nor is it shocking that laws against sexual violence have failed to prevent rape. Rapists don't respect women—why would they respect the law? But there's a good argument that requiring witnesses to report sexual violence to police when they see it might actually make a difference in reducing incidence rates.

It's hard to know what the impact of such a law might be because in the few states that have such laws, such as Massachusetts, the crime of failing to report a crime is almost never enforced, partly because it's a tough crime to uncover, but also because civil libertarians complain that it offends individual liberty to require people to do anything to further the efforts of law enforcement.

Naysayers also will complain that we can't expect people to "snitch" on each other because the risk of retaliation is too great, and because they have to remain silent in order to survive in their communities. One study found that the Los Angeles County district attorney investigated 1,600 cases of witness intimidation, a number that has grown consistently in recent years. In more than 1,000 gang-violence cases, witnesses refused to cooperate.

But citizens have a right and a duty to testify in judicial proceedings. If a person is summoned to appear in court and doesn't show up, he or she can be arrested and sent to jail.

The system itself, not the police and prosecutors, has a right to insist on "everyman's evidence." It isn't fascism, it's democracy in action.

It would be even better if we could encourage more direct bystander intervention, and not just criminalize the nonreporting of crime. But it's a lot to ask folks to put themselves in harm's way for the protection of others and the good of society—even though we expect firefighters, cops, and people in the military to do it every day for little compensation.

And there's always a risk that encouraging witnesses to get personally involved in crime prevention will breed vigilantism. But most data from Crime Stopper types of organizations and neighborhood watch programs suggest the opposite is true. More involvement by citizens tends to increase the social stigma associated with unlawful behavior—which helps reduce crime.

I'm not saying we should all take *CSI* training and start snooping on each other about every suspicious thing we see and hear. But we know that mandatory child-abuse reporting laws help to protect kids by obligating nonoffending adults to file a report with protective-services agencies when there are "reasonable grounds" to believe that a child is being neglected or abused. If we can make a phone call when we *think* a child is in danger, is it too much to ask that we do the same thing when we *know* firsthand that a human being of any age is being brutalized?

> "When you find out that someone you
> know is a pedophile, that doesn't erase
> your knowledge that they're also a hu-
> man being."

Nonintervening Witnesses of Sexual Violence Should Not Be Punished

Megan McArdle

In the following viewpoint, Megan McArdle, a senior editor at the Atlantic Monthly, *challenges arguments that when someone witnesses one person harming another, the witness is compelled to intervene. She discusses criticisms of Penn State coaches Joe Paterno and Mike McQueary, who knew that fellow coach Jerry Sandusky was sexually abusing children but did not report him. McArdle argues that stopping, or reporting, such abuse is much more difficult and complex than many realize or admit. While McArdle concedes that it is wrong to ignore abuse like Sandusky's, doing so does not make someone inhuman.*

As you read, consider the following questions:

1. How many gentiles actually sheltered Jews in Nazi Germany, according to McArdle's source?

Megan McArdle, "The Real Problem at Penn State," *The Atlantic,* November 14, 2011. Copyright © 2011 by The Atlantic. All rights reserved. Republished with permission.

2. What is the scientific term referred to by the author for people without emotional bonds to others?

3. In McArdle's view, how should people encourage each other to do the right thing?

I have been thinking some more about the Penn State case [in which then-assistant football coach Jerry Sandusky sexually assaulted at least eight boys in the program for troubled youth that he founded, The Second Mile], and why [his colleague Mike] McQueary [who witnessed Sandusky assaulting a boy in 2002 and reported it] and [head coach Joe] Paterno did what they did. And I have come to the conclusion that most commentators are overlooking a rather obvious contributing factor: they liked Sandusky.

McQueary grew up in State College [Pennsylvania, home of Penn State]; his family was friends with Sandusky, and of course, Sandusky had coached him. Paterno had worked with Sandusky closely for years. And if you think about what you would have done in a situation where you caught someone you love and respect in that position, is it really so obvious, as the chest thumping punditariat [media commentators] proclaims, that you would have leaped into the shower, beaten the snot out of him, and frog marched him to the police station after you rescued the kid? Really? You'd have done that to your father, your favorite uncle, your best friend, a beloved mentor?

Think about what that really entails: overcoming all the shock and horror, the defensive mechanisms that make you question what you're really seeing. The total destruction of a long relationship as soon as you name it out loud and accuse him to his face. The actual physical logistics of grabbing a naked sixty year old man, detaching him from that child, and then pounding on him for a while as a ten year old you don't know watches. The fact that the minute you go to the police, you will have utterly ruined this man's life: he will be jobless, friendless, and branded as the worst sort of pervert by everyone in the country—oh, and also, in protective custody so that the other inmates in jail don't, like, kill him.

A Blithe Response

That's a pretty huge emotional hurdle to leap in the ten seconds or so that McQueary had to do the right thing. Isn't it quite understandable that your instinct might be to get away? To look for some way that didn't have to involve jail? Wouldn't it be a huge relief to tell your superiors and let someone else take care of it?

[Political commentator] Andrew Sullivan listens to a similar argument from a reader, and dismisses it:

> Yes it f---ing does. If you see anyone—even your own father—raping a ten year old in the showers, the first thing you do is stop it yourself. You don't even call the cops right away. You clock the rapist in the head or drag the boy out of his clutches. I'm so sick of these excuses for the inexcusable. McQueary is as depraved as all the others who stood by and did nothing.

I think Andrew is quite right about the right thing to do in that situation. But I find this rather blithe.

Have you ever polled your friends about how many of them would have been sheltering Jews in Nazi Germany? In the casual conversations I've had, the percentage of people who say that they would of course have helped runs somewhere between 85 and 95%. Actual number: about 10,000, according to Yad Vashem [Israeli Holocaust memorial and research center]. Of course, that number is incomplete, and includes only those who actually risked their lives. But multiply it by 10; multiply it by 100. You're still at what, 1% of the people who had the opportunity to defy the Nazis as they accomplished the most comprehensive ethnic cleansing in history?

> ## Not a Helpful Strategy
>
> Do we want a society in which people who see a crime but don't report it to the police become criminalized? If you see a mugging and don't report it immediately to the police you are morally bankrupt but not a criminal. . . . Snitching is the right thing to do in every conceivable sense if you see a child being sodomized, but to create another class of criminals for not snitching doesn't seem helpful.
>
> *Barbara Amiel,* Maclean's, *November 29, 2011.*

Was this because 99% of Germans, Poles, French, Dutch, and other peoples were "depraved"? Or were they frightened people in a brutal state, with rather ordinary levels of cowardice and indifference to the plight of others?

Never Underestimate Group Loyalty

Oh, well, that's an extreme example, you may say; McQueary was at no risk of life and limb. Fair enough, but one can name dozens of less dangerous situations where only a small minority actually does the right thing, but everyone believes that they woulda. Consider, for example, child abuse (sexual or otherwise) in families. How often is the offender actually reported to the police, and how often do the families simply keep the kids away from Grandpa because, well, *you* know. I'm sure at some level they worry about other kids Grandpa might be touching—but they also worry about what would happen to Grandpa in jail, and the rest of his family in the court of public opinion.

When you find out that someone you know is a pedophile, that doesn't erase your knowledge that they're also a human being. It does in the public mind, of course, but it's very different when you know them.

We are evolved to live in small groups, with very deep loyalty to the other members. In most situations, this is in fact a completely laudable sentiment. But this is the dark side: it is very hard for us to betray the members of those small groups to which we belong, particularly if we have strong emotional bonds to that person. There is a scientific name for people who are not bound by these sorts of ties: sociopaths. And as I understand it, they do not, in fact, make excellent agents of justice, because they don't care about the victims, either.

Easier Said than Done

Every time some group protects one of its own, there is a chorus of shock and horror at the unthinkable venality of cops protecting other cops who fix parking tickets, or gang members who won't snitch, or doctors who close ranks around a borderline incompetent doctor. And yet, my sense is that these same people are often quite sympathetic to the excesses of personal and group loyalty . . . in groups they belong to. When [British author] EM Forster said, "I hate the idea of causes, and if I had to choose between betraying my country and betraying my friend, I hope I should have the guts to betray my country," the implication was rather stupid and horrible (especially since he said it when war with Nazi Germany was looming for his country) . . . and yet, it says something very real about the way humans actually act.

Thus when I hear everyone confidently proclaiming that they would have done the right thing in McQueary's place, I am suspicious that this is actually true. It's easy for all of us to imagine pounding Sandusky because he's a much-reviled stranger. But he wasn't, to McQueary. He was someone he liked, respected, maybe even loved.

Wrong, but Comprehensible

Can you really be so sure that you'd have stepped in right then? Can you honestly say that you've never cut slack for people you like and respect, and maybe people who also happen to have some impact on your career?

You've never kept silent while they were doing something that you were pretty sure was really wrong? I'm not talking about looting the company coffers or molesting children, necessarily—maybe it's the friend who cheated on his wife, or the one who's occasionally rather nasty to his children, or I don't know, a political administration who you like but who also does some stuff that is really pretty bad. If you have found yourself making excuses to let them—or yourself—slide, then you know basically how McQueary felt.

That doesn't excuse what McQueary did. His reaction may be common, but it was still wrong. And we encourage others to do the right thing by forcefully declaring what that right thing is, and shaming those who fail to live up to even a very difficult standard.

An Unhelpful Categorization

But categorizing his act as depraved and incomprehensible is unhelpful. It's unfortunately normal, and entirely comprehensible. Saying otherwise allows us to write off what happened at Penn State to evil people, or a "culture" full of nasty, macho football lovers. It allows us to avoid confronting the real problem, which is that people are evolved to form intense bonds that often trump more abstract principles . . . and also, to be very good at coming up with excuses for not doing what they should at great personal cost to themselves.

Of course, that's not neat and convenient: we don't get to think that the problem is localized to far off people who are nothing like our wonderful friends and relations. But I think it's perhaps more likely to help us prevent such happenings in our own backyard.

"The effects of childhood sexual abuse often span a lifetime. The opportunity to seek justice should last just as long."

There Should Be No Statute of Limitations on Child Sexual Abuse

Jon Wertheim

In the following viewpoint, Jon Wertheim, a senior writer at Sports Illustrated, *argues that there should be no statute of limitations for child sex abuse cases. Under most state laws, once abuse victims reach a certain age, their perpetrators can no longer be charged. While these statutes make sense for other crimes, Wertheim contends, the nature of sex abuse often delays victims' recognition of what has happened to them and summoning the courage to confront their abusers. He cites several cases where adults who were abused as children finally came forward, only to be told that nothing could be done.*

As you read, consider the following questions:

1. What is the statute of limitations for civil child sex abuse cases in New York State, according to Wertheim?

Jon Wertheim, "End Statute of Limitations on Child Sex Crimes," *CNN Wire*, December 16, 2011. Reproduced by permission.

2. What are some of the reasons that statutes of limitations exist for most crimes, according to the author?

3. What are some of the groups Wertheim refers to that object to suspending the statute of limitations for child sex abuse?

The Penn State scandal [in which then-assistant football coach Jerry Sandusky sexually assaulted at least eight boys in the program for troubled youth he founded, The Second Mile] was just starting to reach a rolling boil last month [November 2011] when the Department of Education announced that it would be investigating the school for a possible violation of the Clery Act. A quarter century ago [1986], Jeanne Clery was asleep in her Lehigh University dorm room when she was raped and killed by an intruder.

The act came about after Clery's parents discovered that more than three dozen violent crimes had been committed on the campus over the three years before their daughter's murder; yet administrators didn't see fit to disclose this information. In 1990, Congress passed the Jeanne Clery Disclosure of Campus Security Policy and Campus Crime Statistics Act, requiring that schools that receive federal funds report crime statistics and make timely warnings to the campus community about crimes that pose a threat to students and employees.

Often it takes a tragedy to establish or improve public policy.

So it is that the recent flurry of high-profile child sex abuse scandals will surely trigger change and reform. We can start here: suspending the statute of limitations in these types of cases.

Statutes Are Common

Laws vary among states, but in most cases, when victims reach a certain age, perpetrators can no longer be charged with these crimes, nor can the accusers seek remedies in civil court.

The statute of limitations in New York for bringing civil claims for child sex abuse is five years after it was reported to police or five years after the victim turns 18. That was also the standard for criminal prosecutions, until it was lifted altogether in 2008 for first-degree rape, aggravated sexual abuse and course of sexual conduct against a child.

In Pennsylvania, the criminal statute of limitations extends until the victim reaches the age of 50. But child sex abuse victims must file civil suits before they turn 30—and the law was enacted in August 2002, so survivors who turned 20 before the law was enacted are barred from suing their perpetrators.

How does this apply to the recent cases in Penn State and Syracuse [in which former Syracuse University assistant basketball coach Bernie Fine was accused of sexually abusing two ball boys]? If a victim of Jerry Sandusky was born before 1982, he is likely time-barred from bringing action against the disgraced former Penn State football coach. (Given that it was in 1977 that Sandusky established the Second Mile Foundation—the organization through which, prosecutors allege, he cultivated relationships with victims—this is significant.)

In Syracuse, despite finding the allegations to be credible, prosecutors have already declined to pursue criminal sex abuse charges against former assistant basketball coach Bernie Fine. Why? Because the men accusing Fine of molestation in the 1980s are well into adulthood, and the statute of limitations has long since lapsed.

A Different Kind of Crime

There are various reasons why we have statutes of limitations for crimes, other than the worst felonies, and for torts [non-criminal actions that cause someone harm]. Memories fade. Witnesses die. Evidence goes bad. We want to encourage plaintiffs to bring suit as quickly after the alleged injury as possible. Potential defendants should be able to get on with their lives without worrying about getting charged or sued for acts al-

A Troubled Silence

Young adults, particularly men, who suffer the aftereffects of abuse are rarely in an emotional state to bring charges. Given what we now know about why it takes victims so long to come forward, the law [child sexual abuse statute of limitation] needs to be changed.

Many people cast a skeptical eye on those who wait so long to reveal instances of child abuse, particularly when it happened to them as teenagers. They assume that accusers are making it up, blaming what were at most minor incidents for their troubles.

But in my decades of experience working with abuse victims, I have found that men spend years putting their emotions in a deep freeze or masking post-traumatic reactions with self-defeating behaviors like compulsive gambling and substance abuse. Eventually, they are forced by internal or external events to find treatment.

Richard B. Gartner, New York Times, *June 7, 2012.*

leged from long ago. If anyone could sue anyone at anytime it would further clog an already congested legal system. In most cases, this all makes sense.

Not so for child sexual abuse. The very nature of the crime is predicated on secrecy and shame and manipulation. It often takes years, decades even, for victims to grasp what has happened: that an adult, often a trusted authority figure or a family member, did horribly wrong by them.

Regardless of the guilt or innocence of Sandusky or Fine, the obvious complexity and ambiguity of the relationships they had with their accusers, as well as the intense public fallout in the wake of the allegations, offer graphic examples of why alleged victims might feel disabled well into adulthood. Shutting the door on accusers only serves to arm the molesters with still another advantage in what is already an unfair fight.

A Deeply Guarded Secret

Tammy Lerner knows this first hand. Now 41, she maintains that, as a young girl growing up in Union County, Pennsylvania, she was raped by a favorite relative.

Conflicted, ashamed, scared to risk fraying the tapestry of her tight-knit family, she held it as a deeply guarded secret. In the late '90s, she felt that she could no longer stay quiet.

As it turned out, several of her cousins claimed to have had similar experiences. Together, they went to the local prosecutor, only to be told they had been time-barred. "It was just that he wasn't brought to justice," says Lerner, who went on to found the Foundation to Abolish Sex Abuse, Inc. "When he wasn't charged and there could be no civil case, he couldn't be named publically. . . . Worse than injustice for victims is the paralysis and guilt that we feel over not being able to spare a new generation of kids the horrors of abuse that we experienced as children."

Laws Favor Predators

Over the objections of numerous groups—insurance lobbies, teachers unions, Roman Catholic clergymen—some states have decided to suspend the statute of limitations for these crimes, a tacit recognition of the unique dynamics of child sex crimes. Delaware recently [2007] suspended the statute of limitations for two years, creating a window for those previously time-barred to come forward. More than 100 alleged victims emerged.

In California, a similar suspension spurred more than 300 lawsuits, some dating back to episodes from the 1950s. "It's clear that it can take a long, long time before victims are ready to confront abuse and everything that can come with it," says Marci Hamilton, a law professor at Cardozo Law School and a lawyer for one of the accusers in the Sandusky case. "It's just wrong to have [policy] that favors the predator."

A vast body of research indicates that the effects of childhood sexual abuse often span a lifetime. The opportunity to seek justice should last just as long.

Periodical and Internet Sources Bibliography

The following articles have been selected to supplement the diverse views presented in this chapter.

Barbara Amiel	"This Isn't the Way to Protect Our Children," *Maclean's*, December 5, 2011.
Richard B. Gartner	"A Troubled Silence," *New York Times*, June 7, 2012.
Jessica Grose	"Why Are There Statutes of Limitations in Child Rape Cases?," *Slate*, December 21, 2011. www.slate.com.
Amanda Hess	"Can Twitter Help Rape Victims Find Justice?," *Slate*, July 23, 2012. www.slate.com.
Juliette Kayye	"Women in Combat Are Not a Cause of Sexual Assault, but Could Be the Cure," *Boston Globe*, July 16, 2012.
New Statesman	"We Must Not Dismiss or Diminish Allegations of Rape," August 24, 2012.
Xiaofan Pan	"Holding Campuses Accountable in Reporting Sexual Assault," *Women's Health Activist*, July–August 2012.
Jeff Parrott	"Getting Through? How Catholic Campuses Are Responding to Sexual Assault," *U.S. Catholic*, January 2012.
Thomas Plante	"Do the Right Thing," *Psychology Today*, June 11, 2012.
Women in Higher Education	"Male Peer Educators Can Reduce Campus Sexual Violence," February 2010.
Jan Wong	"What Evil Lurks," *Toronto Life*, October 2010.

For Further Discussion

Chapter 1

1. Heather Mac Donald sees Mary Koss's study of rape on college campuses as implicitly flawed because "73% of the women whom the study characterized as rape victims told the researchers that they hadn't been raped." Do you agree with Mac Donald that the subjects' interpretations of their experiences invalidate the study's conclusions? Why or why not?

2. According to Jessica A. Turchik and Susan M. Wilson, several different studies have determined that sexual assault is more common in the US military than in the general public. If this is indeed true, what might be the reasons?

Chapter 2

1. In his viewpoint, George Weigel uses the phrase "Catholic Lite," saying at one point that it "is not the answer to what has essentially been a crisis of fidelity." What do you think Weigel means by "Catholic Lite"? Do you think he would put this label on Fran Ferder and John Heagle's argument? Why or why not?

2. Both Gail Dines and Todd D. Kendall assert that pornography influences rates of sexual assault; Dines believes pornography encourages rape while Kendall believes it may discourage it. But, according to Dines, pornographers frequently argue "that pornography has no effect on its consumers." Do you think this is possible, or do you agree with Dines and Kendall that pornography necessarily influences consumers one way or the other? Explain.

Chapter 3

1. While the *National Catholic Reporter* viewpoint harshly criticizes Pope Benedict XVI for his lack of honesty and transparency during the Catholic Church sex abuse scandal, Brian Bethune's viewpoint points out how much more honest and transparent Benedict was than Pope John Paul II, his predecessor. To what extent do you think this context should be taken into account when judging Benedict's handling of the scandal? Explain your answer.

2. Joseph Shapiro explains that "campus disciplinary programs are not set up like a court of law. . . . Schools see the role of these courts to teach students more than to mete out justice," which is why punishments are often so light. Do you think campus courts ought to operate more like courts of law, with more focus on justice and less on education? Why or why not?

3. To Marisa Taylor and Chris Adams, the fact that military commanders, rather than prosecutors, decide whether to press charges appears problematic. Can you think of some advantage to this procedure or reasons it may have been implemented in the first place? Explain.

Chapter 4

1. Wendy Murphy says that "we need better ways of incentivizing bystanders to give a damn" and that "without some legal ramification for such interpersonal inertia, doing nothing will always be the preferred path of least resistance for many people." Do you agree that passive bystander behavior is inevitable and unchangeable in most people, or do you think it is an effect of culture, and thus, subject to change? Explain your answer, citing from the viewpoints.

2. Jon Wertheim makes the case that statutes of limitations should be ended for child sex abuse cases because "the very nature of the crime is predicated on secrecy and

shame and manipulation. It often takes years, decades even, for victims to grasp what has happened." But much, or perhaps all, of this reasoning could also be applied to other forms of sexual violence. Do you think the statute of limitations should be eliminated for these crimes as well? Why or why not?

Organizations to Contact

The editors have compiled the following list of organizations concerned with the issues debated in this book. The descriptions are derived from materials provided by the organizations. All have publications or information available for interested readers. The list was compiled on the date of publication of the present volume; the information provided here may change. Be aware that many organizations take several weeks or longer to respond to inquiries, so allow as much time as possible.

Amnesty International USA
5 Penn Plaza, New York, NY   10001
(212) 807-8400 • fax: (212) 627-1451
e-mail: aimember@aiusa.org
website: www.amnestyusa.org

Amnesty International is a research, activist, and advocacy organization that seeks to unite people all over the world to fight for the human rights of all of the world's citizens. Amnesty addresses issues such as poverty, the death penalty, refugee and migrant rights, torture, women's rights, and free speech. Among its numerous publications are reports such as *Hidden from Justice: Impunity for Conflict-Related Sexual Violence in Colombia* and *The Gender Trap: Women, Violence and Poverty*, as well as the blog *Human Rights Now*.

BishopAccountability.org
PO Box 541375, Waltham, MA   02454-1375
(508) 479-9304
e-mail: staff@bishopaccountability.org
website: www.bishop-accountability.org

BishopAccountability.org is an educational nonprofit organization with the goal of facilitating the accountability of US Catholic bishops for their roles in the church sexual abuse crisis. The organization does not advocate for any particular remedy for the crisis but simply provides an archive of every publicly available document and report on the crisis. Its publications include the *Abuse Tracker* blog and the *Monitor* newsletter.

Darkness to Light (D2L)

7 Radcliffe Street, Suite 200, Charleston, SC   29403
(843) 965-5444 • fax: (843) 965-5449
e-mail: stewards@d2l.org
website: www.d2l.org

Darkness to Light's single mission is to end child sexual abuse through public awareness and education. The organization provides programs that train individuals and organizations to prevent, recognize, and appropriately respond to childhood sex abuse. D2L publishes guides such as *7 Steps to Protecting Our Children* and *A Parent's Guide to Selecting Youth Serving Organizations*, as well as the *Darkness to Light Blog*.

Just Detention International (JDI)

3325 Wilshire Blvd., Suite 340, Los Angeles, CA   90010
(213) 384-1400 • fax: (213) 384-1411
e-mail: info@justdetention.org
website: www.justdetention.org

Just Detention International is a health and human rights organization with the goal of ending sexual assault in all places of detention, including prisons, jails, juvenile facilities, and halfway houses. JDI advocates for the well-being of inmates, holds officials accountable, promotes public understanding, and provides resources to survivors. The organization publishes *Action Update, PREA Update*, fact sheets such as "Sexual Abuse in U.S. Immigration Detention," and reports such as "Improving Prison Oversight to Address Sexual Violence in Prison."

Men Can Stop Rape

1003 K Street NW, Suite 200, Washington, DC   20001
(202) 265-6530 • fax: (202) 265-4362

e-mail: info@mencanstoprape.org
website: www.mencanstoprape.org

Men Can Stop Rape was founded in order to shift the responsibility for deterring sexual violence away from women by promoting a healthy masculinity in men. The organization provides public awareness campaigns, as well as educational and training programs for youth, college-age men, and youth-serving organizations. Its publications include the *Where Do You Stand?* campaign guide and information sheets such as "Stopping Rape: What Male Athletes Can Do" and "Defining the Rules Between Sex and Rape."

National Sexual Violence Resource Center (NSVRC)
123 N. Enola Drive, Enola, PA   17025
(717) 909-0710 • fax: (717) 909-0714
e-mail: resources@nsvrc.org
website: www.nsvrc.org

The National Sexual Violence Resource Center serves as a national resource hub for all aspects of sexual violence. It collects and disseminates information to coalitions; rape crisis centers; national, state, and local agencies; and other organizations devoted to preventing and responding to sexual violence. The NSVRC publishes a newsletter, the *Resource*, fact sheets such as the "Human Trafficking Overview," guides such as *Sexual Harassment & Bullying of Youth*, as well as many other publications.

Office on Violence Against Women (OVW)
US Department of Justice, Washington, DC   20530
(202) 307-6026 • fax: (202) 305-2589
website: www.ovw.usdoj.gov

The Office on Violence Against Women, a component of the US Department of Justice, provides federal leadership in addressing and reducing violence against women, including domestic violence, dating violence, sexual assault, and stalking. The OVW administers financial and technical assistance to communities across the United States that are developing programs, policies, and practices for ending violence against women. Among the office's publications are the "Report on September 2011 Sexual Violence Research Roundtable," the *National Protocol for Sexual Assault Medical Forensic Examinations,* and *Civil Protection Orders: A Guide for Improving Practice.*

Rape, Abuse & Incest National Network (RAINN)
1220 L Street NW, Suite 505, Washington, DC 20005
(202) 544-3064; hotline: (800) 656-4673 • fax: (202) 544-3556
e-mail: info@rainn.org
website: www.rainn.org

RAINN is the largest anti-sexual-violence organization in the United States. The organization operates the National Sexual Assault Hotline; provides information and other resources to policy makers, the media, law enforcement personnel, and others; and provides programs aimed at preventing sexual violence and helping victims. RAINN publishes a monthly e-newsletter, as well as periodic press releases and statements on issues related to sexual violence.

Service Women's Action Network (SWAN)
220 E. Twenty-Third Street, Suite 509, New York, NY 10010
(646) 569-5200 • fax: (646) 383-9495
e-mail: info@servicewomen.org
website: www.servicewomen.org

The Service Women's Action Network is a nonpartisan civil rights organization working to transform military culture so that women have equal opportunity to serve without discrimination, harassment, and assault and so that women veterans and their families have access to high-quality health care and benefits. SWAN pursues its mission through media advocacy, litigation, direct services, and policy reform. Among its publications are fact sheets such as "Women in Combat" and "Rape, Sexual Assault, and Sexual Harassment in the Military—the Quick Facts," as well as a newsletter and blog.

Sexual Assault Prevention and Response Office (SAPRO)

US Department of Defense, Washington, DC   20301-1400
(571) 372-2657
e-mail: sapro@sapr.mil
website: www.sapr.mil

SAPRO is the organization responsible for the oversight of the US Department of Defense's sexual assault policy. Its main aims are to prevent sexual assault in the military, to provide appropriate treatment and support for sexual assault victims, and to ensure system accountability. SAPRO publishes annual reports on the status of sexual assault in the US military, research reports such as "2011 Sexual Assault Gender Relations Focus Groups Report," and training materials for active bystanders, service members, commanders, and civilians.

Students Active for Ending Rape (SAFER)

32 Broadway, Suite 1101, New York, NY   10004
(347) 465-7233
website: www.safercampus.org

SAFER is an all-volunteer organization that seeks to empower student-led campaigns to reform college sexual assault policies. It facilitates student organizing through training and workshops, activist mentoring, and resource dissemination. SAFER publishes *Change Happens: A Guide to Reforming Your Campus Sexual Assault Policy*.

Survivors Network of Those Abused by Priests (SNAP)

PO Box 6416, Chicago, IL   60680-6416
(312) 455-1499 • fax: (312) 455-1498
website: www.snapnetwork.org

SNAP is an independent network of survivors of religious sexual abuse and their supporters. Its goals include exposing and bringing to justice sexual predators, healing sexual abuse survivors, and preventing future abuse. SNAP publishes a blog and periodic media releases.

Bibliography of Books

Irina Anderson
and Kathy
Doherty, eds.

Accounting for Rape. New York:
Routledge, 2008.

Nader Baydoun
and R. Stephanie
Good

*A Rush to Injustice: How Power,
Prejudice, Racism, and Political
Correctness Overshadowed Truth and
Justice in the Duke Lacrosse Rape
Case*. Nashville, TN: Thomas Nelson,
2007.

Jeff Benedict

*Out of Bounds: Inside the NBA's
Culture of Rape, Violence, and Crime*.
New York: It Books, 2005.

Joanna Bourke

Rape: Sex, Violence, History. Berkeley,
CA: Counterpoint, 2007.

Anne-Marie de
Brouwer and
Sandra Ka
Hon-Chu, eds.

*The Men Who Killed Me: Rwandan
Survivors of Sexual Violence*.
Vancouver, BC: Douglas & McIntyre,
2009.

Anne-Marie de
Brouwer,
Charlotte Ku,
Renee Romkens,
Larissa van den
Herik, eds.

*Sexual Violence as an International
Crime: Interdisciplinary Approaches*.
Cambridge, UK: Intersentia, 2012.

Kristin Bumiller

*In an Abusive State: How
Neoliberalism Appropriated the
Feminist Movement Against Sexual
Violence*. Durham, NC: Duke
University Press, 2008.

Charli Carpenter, ed. — *Born of War: Protecting Children of Sexual Violence Survivors in Conflict Zones.* Sterling, VA: Kumarian, 2007.

Walter S. DeKeseredy — *Violence Against Women: Myths, Facts, Controversies.* Toronto: University of Toronto Press, 2011.

Randy Ellison — *Boys Don't Tell: Ending the Silence of Abuse.* New York: Morgan James, 2011.

Patti Feuereisen with Caroline Pincus — *Invisible Girls: The Truth About Sexual Abuse.* Berkeley, CA: Seal Press, 2005.

Bonnie S. Fisher, Leah E. Daigle, Francis T. Cullen — *Unsafe in the Ivory Tower: The Sexual Victimization of College Women.* Thousand Oaks, CA: Sage, 2009.

Mark S. Fleisher and Jessie L. Krienert — *The Myth of Prison Rape: Sexual Culture in American Prisons.* Lanham, MD: Rowman & Littlefield, 2009.

Nicola Gavey — *Just Sex? The Cultural Scaffolding of Rape.* New York: Routledge, 2005.

Sarah D. Goode — *Understanding and Addressing Adult Sexual Attraction to Children: A Study of Paedophiles in Contemporary Society.* New York: Routledge, 2009.

Carol Harrington — *Politicization of Sexual Violence.* Burlington, VT: Ashgate, 2010.

Renee J. Heberle and Victoria Grace, eds. — *Theorizing Sexual Violence.* New York: Routledge, 2009.

Elizabeth D. Heineman, ed. — *Sexual Violence in Conflict Zones: From the Ancient World to the Era of Human Rights*. Philadelphia: University of Pennsylvania Press, 2011.

Jessica Alison Hubbard — *Understanding Rape as Genocide: A Feminist Analysis of Sexual Violence and Genocide*. Saarbrucken, Germany: Akademikerverlag, 2012.

Mic Hunter — *Honor Betrayed: Sexual Abuse in America's Military*. Fort Lee, NJ: Barricade Books, 2007.

Catherine Itzin, Ann Taket, Sarah Barter-Godfrey — *Domestic and Sexual Violence and Abuse: Tackling the Health and Mental Health Effects*. New York: Routledge, 2010.

Helen Jones and Kate Cook — *Rape Crisis: Responding to Sexual Violence*. Dorset, UK: Russell House, 2008.

Kathleen Kuehnast, Chantal de Jonge Oudraat, Helga Hernes, eds. — *Women and War: Power and Protection in the 21st Century*. Washington, DC: US Institute of Peace Press, 2011.

Sally Engle Merry — *Gender Violence: A Cultural Perspective*. Hoboken, NJ: Wiley-Blackwell, 2008.

Nick T. Pappas — *The Dark Side of Sports: Exposing the Sexual Culture of Collegiate and Professional Athletes*. Indianapolis, IN: Meyer & Meyer Sport, 2012.

Joshua Daniel Phillips	*1,800 Miles: Striving to End Sexual Violence, One Step at a Time.* New York: Morgan James, 2010.
Jordan A. Prescott and Adrian M. Madsen, eds.	*Sexual Violence in Africa's Conflict Zones.* Hauppauge, NY: Nova Science, 2011.
Joshua M. Price	*Structural Violence: Hidden Brutality in the Lives of Women.* Albany: SUNY Press, 2012.
James Ptacek, ed.	*Restorative Justice and Violence Against Women.* New York: Oxford University Press, 2009.
John K. Roth and Carol Rittner	*Rape: Weapon of War and Genocide.* St. Paul, MN: Paragon House, 2012.
Peggy Reeves Sanday	*Fraternity Gang Rape: Sex, Brotherhood, and Privilege on Campus.* New York: NYU Press, 2007.
Todd K. Shackelford and Aaron T. Goetz, eds.	*The Oxford Handbook of Sexual Conflict in Humans.* New York: Oxford University Press, 2012.
Sara Sharratt	*Gender, Shame, and Sexual Violence.* Burlington, VT: Ashgate, 2011.
Andrew L. Spivak	*Sexual Violence: Beyond the Feminist-Evolutionary Debate.* El Paso, TX: LFB Scholarly, 2011.
Tonia St. Germain and Susan Dewey, eds.	*Conflict-Related Sexual Violence: International Law, Local Responses.* Sterling, VA: Kumarian, 2012.

William M. Struthers	*Wired for Intimacy: How Pornography Hijacks the Male Brain.* Nottingham, UK: IVP Books, 2009.
Jaqui True	*The Political Economy of Violence Against Women.* New York: Oxford University Press, 2012.
Sarah E. Ullman	*Talking About Sexual Assault: Society's Response to Survivors.* Washington, DC: American Psychological Association, 2010.
Laura J. Zilney and Lisa Anne Zilney	*Perverts and Predators: The Making of Sexual Offending Laws.* Lanham, MD: Rowman & Littlefield, 2009.

Index